HOT CARS!

HOT CARS!

An Inside Look at the Auto Theft Industry

by
Marcus Wayne Ratledge

Paladin Press
Boulder, Colorado

Hot Cars!
An Inside Look at the Auto Theft Industry
by Marcus Wayne Ratledge
Copyright © 1982 by Marcus Wayne Ratledge

ISBN 0-87364-220-1
Printed in the United States of America

Published by Paladin Press, a division of
Paladin Enterprises, Inc., P.O. Box 1307,
Boulder, Colorado 80306, USA.
(303) 443-7250

Direct inquiries and/or orders to the above address.

Library of Congress Cataloging in Publication Data

Ratledge, Marcus Wayne
    Hot Cars!

    1. Automobile theft.   I. Title
HV6652. R37   364.1'62   81-18781
ISBN 0-87364-220-1   AACR2

To Allen and Bobby

Contents

Introduction

Changeover is criminal trade jargon for the conversion of unlawfully obtained automobiles, trucks, motorcycles, pickup trucks, vans, motorcycles, camping and travel trailers, boats, and even airplanes into transportation that can be sold, traded, or driven without anyone realizing that they are not of legitimate origin. Changeover is a catchall term that also includes stripping cars and trucks of their parts for reuse.

The changeover industry is one I know well. For more than twenty years my primary business was stealing, stripping, converting, and selling vehicles of all kinds. As a teen-ager, I worked in a "chop shop" dismantling stolen autos and delivering the parts to so-called legitimate body repair shops. As I grew older, I moved into the stealing phase of the business and for four years stole automobiles on an exact order basis. These vehicles were either stripped for their parts or converted to legally papered transportation and sold on the retail market. In later years I organized and managed my own theft operations and expanded into the theft of vehicles other than automobiles.

During my career, I personally stole more than twelve hundred automobiles, trucks, trailers, motorcycles, boats, and even a few airplanes. I also was directly responsible for the theft of at least double that amount and the conversion of all to legitimate transportation.

My career has not been without its mistakes, however. I have been to prison three times for auto theft where I served a total of five years and three months. But I learned from my mistakes and have not had a conviction for a charge related to the changeover industry since I was nineteen years old.

I am writing this book while serving a prison sentence for an unrelated charge. Since my confinement, I have realized the senselessness of my misdeeds and am planning a substantially different course for my life upon my release. My first book, *Don't Become The Victim*, published by Paladin Press, tells how the criminal mind works, where the criminal is most likely to strike, what his methods are, and how he can be defeated.

In an effort to rectify some of the harm and frustrations I have caused so many people over the years, especially law enforcement agencies, I decided to write this book as an exposé of the highly profitable, criminal industry I once helped build. In doing so, I have revealed every trick of the trade I know. These successful deceptions have placed millions of stolen vehicles on the streets of America and other countries worldwide, and billions of dollars in the pockets of the thieves who practiced them.

This book is intended to serve as a guide to law enforcement agencies, state title and registration offices, insurance companies, automotive and recreational vehicle dealerships, salvage yards, motorcycle shops, Federal Aviation Agency and airport personnel, and marinas in detecting stolen vehicles and recognizing the operational patterns of changeover artists. Lawmakers will be able to see the loopholes in present title and registration laws that permit the changeover industry to flourish.

Potential buyers of a car, truck, van, motorcycle, camper or recreational vehicle, boat, or airplane will find simple procedures for making certain that they will never find themselves in possession of a stolen vehicle.

1 Dispelling the Myths

There are a few myths about the changeover industry that should be put to rest once and for all in order to separate fact from fantasy.

Myth number one: Most auto theft is controlled by the Mafia.

False. There is a tendency to attribute every organized criminal endeavor to the Mafia, just as it was once fashionable to attribute racial violence only to the Ku Klux Klan. Undoubtedly, the Mafia is active in the auto theft business, but its operations are limited to a few cities along the eastern seaboard where it has traditionally ruled for decades.

The majority of changeover operations are small, locally owned and operated businesses. An operation which handles three or more vehicles a day is considered large scale.

Myth number two: The majority of stolen vehicles are never recovered.

False. More than 60 percent of all stolen vehicles are recovered. Those recovered were usually stolen by joy riders out for a thrill, transients wanting a ride from one point to another, amateurs who stripped the vehicle and abandoned it where they thought it would not be found for a few days, and burglars and robbers who used the vehicle to commit a crime.

Myth number three: Autos with locking steering columns are less likely to be stolen.

False. They are more likely to be stolen because they are new. The locking system may deter the joy riders and transients, but a professional car thief can steal any vehicle about as fast as it can be unlocked and started with a key. Besides, the law makes no distinction between the different makes, models, and ages of vehicles when imposing prison terms for their theft. The thief knows he will not be given more time for stealing a new Cadillac than he would for stealing an old Volkswagen.

Myth number four: Stolen autos that are not stripped and are intended for long-term personal use or sale are always repainted another color.

False. If an auto is stolen by a professional for personal use or sale, it is never repainted. Since there are just as many red cars stolen as blue cars, white ones as black ones, and so on, it makes no sense to paint a red car blue, or a white one black. The police can be looking for a stolen blue Ford, for example, and find the stolen red Ford that has been painted blue. Anyone who knows anything at all about autos can tell when an automobile has had a complete color change.

Myth number five: Automotive and recreational dealers always check out the ownership of vehicles they purchase so there is virtually no chance of purchasing a stolen vehicle from a dealership.

False. Although dealerships are avoided by thieves, mainly because they pay such low prices for the vehicles they purchase, it is common for a thief wanting to make a fast buck to hoodwink a dealer with a hot one. Dealers are unbelievably careless when it comes to checking out ownership. They seem to be more interested in whether or not the vehicle is fully paid for than if the seller is the rightful owner.

Myth number six: The thief who steals the vehicle immediately turns it over to another member of the theft ring, collects between five hundred and twelve hundred dollars for his efforts, and has nothing else to do with the operation until he is asked to steal another vehicle.

False. The person who steals the vehicle gets only a small piece of the pie, usually one hundred to one hundred twenty-five dollars. If the myth were true, I could have retired when I was seventeen and still be living off the interest from my money. It is not always possible to keep the actual thief from knowing other members of the ring, although most operators would prefer it. Fact is, the man who steals the vehicle generally has other duties such as dismantling the vehicle or arranging for its sale.

Myth number seven: When a vehicle is declared a total wreck by an insurance company or title agency, it can never be rebuilt.

False. When a vehicle is declared totally wrecked, usually in the case of automobiles, it means the total cost of rebuilding the vehicle is greater than the cost of replacing it with a similar model. For instance, consider that a 1979 Ford Thunderbird is involved in a severe accident and that the cost of repair is estimated at forty-nine hundred dollars. If the value of the auto wreck in its salvage condition is six hundred dollars and the cost of a rental by the owner until the wrecked auto is repaired is three hundred dollars, the insurance company can purchase a similar replacement auto for forty-five hundred dollars on the wholesale market and actually save one hundred dollars! This is computed by adding the cost of repair plus the cost of the rental, and subtracting the salvage value, for a total of forty-six hundred dollars.

Myth number eight: Nontitle states are bigger and better havens for theft operations than title states.

False. When vehicles are stolen for their parts only, it does not matter whether the state is a title state or not; the thief is not going to be seeking legitimate registration papers anyway. When the theft is for conversion into legitimate transportation, titles merely cause minor inconvenience to the thief and give a greater appearance of authenticity to the transaction when the vehicle is sold.

Myth number nine: Converted stolen vehicles are sold for about one-half their true market value.

False. Most converted vehicles are sold for approximately seven-eighths of their true value. This keeps the prospective purchaser from becoming suspicious.

Myth number ten: High-performance and luxury cars are the most likely candidates for conversion after theft.

Once true, now false. Professional thieves learn to adjust to the demands of the public, just as any other successful businessmen do. When high-performance and luxury autos were in great demand, changeover artists filled this demand. But those were in times of $3,000 autos and thirty-cent a gallon gasoline. Today, with the average price for autos at $6,750, and gasoline going for more than a dollar per gallon, the demand is for smaller, more economical transportation. Thieves make no less money since, while the selling prices have doubled, the overhead has remained virtually unchanged.

Myth number eleven: Numbered parts such as the

engine and transmission are traceable and therefore discarded.

False. Only a very green amateur would dispose of an otherwise perfectly good engine just because it is numbered. Only the engine *block* and the transmission *case* are numbered, the valuable internal parts are not. This leaves the thief with two alternatives other than disposal. He can sell the engine and transmission to an associate who can use the internal parts to rebuild other engines and transmissions, or he can purchase new or used legitimate engine blocks and transmission cases and changeover the internal parts from the stolen blocks and cases to the legitimate ones. They can then be sold on the open market without fear of detection.

2 Title and Salvage Laws

When a vehicle rolls off the assembly line, it is given a *bill of origin*, a document comparable to a birth certificate for humans. Listed on the bill of origin are the name, date, and place of manufacture; make; model; year-model; color; physical characteristics, such as two-door, four-door, hardtop, sedan, hatchback, convertible, or T-top; length and number of axles on heavy-duty trucks, camping and travel trailers, boats and boat trailers; and number of engines on airplanes and boats.

Also listed on the bill of origin are the all-important serial numbers. For automobiles there will be four numbers—frame, engine, transmission, and *Vehicle Identification Number*, referred to as the VIN or VIN plate. The VIN plate bears the nationally recognized serial number of a vehicle that appears on the title and registration papers. It is this number, and only this number, that is run through the National Crime Information Center (NCIC) computer in FBI headquarters in Washington, D.C. to determine whether or not the vehicle is stolen.

The bill of origin for camper and travel trailers lists only one serial number, the VIN, which is stamped into

The bill of origin, referred to as the Manufacturer's Statement of Origin (MSO) by car dealers, is issued for each new car and then turned into the state title office in exchange for a title.

the tongue of the frame on the left side, midway between the hitch and the body of the trailer.

Small boats without an engine often have no serial number on their bill of origin, since they do not have a VIN plate. The bill of origin for larger boats that have a VIN plate and boats that have factory-installed engines will list VIN numbers. If a boat has a serial plate, it will be attached to the helm. Boat trailers list their VIN in the same location as do travel and camping trailers.

The bill of origin for heavy-duty trucks such as tractor-trailers, dump trucks, and vans over twelve feet list serial numbers similar to automobiles, but may have additional serial numbers when the trucks are equipped with dual transmissions and axles. Wheelbase and cab size may also be listed.

Pickup trucks and small vans have serial numbers identical to those for automobiles, which will be listed on the bill of origin.

Motorcycles' bills of origin will list the engine, transmission, and frame numbers. The frame number is the VIN and is located on the motorcycle just below the engine.

Airplanes' bills of origin list the Federal Aviation Administration (FAA) registration number painted on both sides of the rear fuselage and the tail section. Engine numbers as well as any factory-installed avionics equipment bearing numbers will also be listed.

No vehicle has a title until it is sold and registered in the individual states. Some states do not have title laws, however, and no vehicle in these states will have a title as long as it is registered there. If a vehicle is registered in a nontitle state, and the owner moves to a title state or sells the vehicle to someone in a title state, a title can be secured for the vehicle in the title state, providing it can meet the requirements of registration in that state.

I, Arthur Pearl, 263 Alpine Street, Anywhere, Oklahoma, do sell this 1980 Oldsmobile Bonneville, brown with a tan top and wire wheels, serial number DL 087364-112167, to Julie Bauman, 8173 First Avenue, Somewhere, Kansas, for the sum of seven thousand eight hundred fifty dollars ($7,850) on this day, October 30, 1981.

Arthur Pearl

A bill of sale is legal evidence that ownership of a car has been transferred. When buying a vehicle, a buyer should make sure that the person selling it is the rightful owner.

The title and registration will be referred to as a unit since title states require both. Disregard the word *title*, however, in references to states that require only registration.

Title States

When an automobile or truck of any kind is bought new from a dealership in a title state, a *bill of sale* is made out by the dealer. The bill of sale is simply a form or paper that specifies the seller, the make, model, and year of the vehicle, serial number, purchaser, selling price, and date of sale.

To validate the signatures, the bill of sale is taken before a notary public who will witness the signing and notarize the document by signing and stamping it with his seal.

The next step is taking the bill of sale and the vehicle's bill of origin to the state title registration office. After checking with NCIC to make certain that the vehicle is not stolen, a title is issued. On the title is the name of the person to whom the vehicle is registered, the person or financial institution loaning the money, who becomes the *lien holder,* and all serial numbers and descriptions pertinent to the identification of the vehicle.

The title is designed to prevent the vehicle from being sold before all liens have been satisfied. Therefore, when the title is issued, it is not held by the person to whom the vehicle is registered, but by the lien holder of the vehicle. Until the vehicle is fully paid for, the lien holder is, in fact, the owner of that vehicle.

The person to whom the vehicle is registered and who has possession of it cannot sell or otherwise dispose of the vehicle until the liens have been removed and the

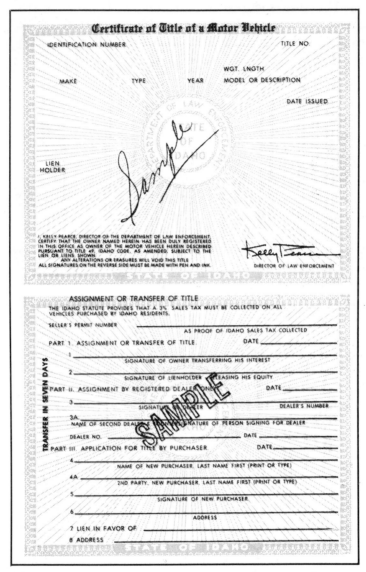

The title shows ownership of a vehicle in title states. It should be kept in a safe place and never left in the vehicle. Title forms vary from state to state and are not issued by nontitle states.

title has been cleared. A clear title can, of course, be obtained at the time of purchase if the vehicle is paid for in full by the purchaser without the use of borrowed money.

After the vehicle is titled, copies of the title and the bill of sale are taken to the license plate registration office. After another NCIC check, license plates and registration papers, better known as the tag receipt or pink slip, are issued in the name of the person who purchased the vehicle.

Whereas the title shows who holds the lien against the vehicle, the registration papers show who owns the vehicle. Unlike the title, the registration papers do not list all of the vehicle's serial numbers. Usually, only the VIN will be listed. In many states, the color of the vehicle is not even listed.

Once the registration procedure is complete, the license plates are placed on the vehicle and the pink slip goes into the glove compartment or over the sun visor. If it is required by the state, the vehicle is also inspected and a safety sticker is placed on the windshield.

Before the vehicle can be sold to another party, the title must be cleared. This can be done by paying off the amount outstanding with a lump sum, through monthly payments (as most of us do), by the dealer when the vehicle is traded in on another vehicle, or by an insurance company in the event the vehicle is totally wrecked or stolen and not recovered.

When the vehicle is sold, the process begins again, except the title is changed into the name of the new lien holder and the registration is changed into the name of the new owner. In some states, the license plates remain with the vehicle until they either expire or the vehicle is permanently laid to rest in a salvage yard. In other states, the license plates are removed when the

ISSUE DATE		**STATE OF IOWA REGISTRATION RENEWAL RECEIPT**			
	DB	CO.	MAKE		**TITLE NO.**
VALID NO./YR.					
		TYPE	YR.		YR.
PLATE NO./YR.					
		T.R.			
WEIGHT					
FEE CODE					
FEE					
PENALTY					
TOTAL					
		COLOR		NEXT FEE	NEXT YR.
OWNER'S COPY		**COUNTY TREASURER**			**SIGNATURE OF OWNER**

EXPLANATION OF "CODE"

V = DISABLED VETERAN M = MILITARY NONRESIDENT (PASSENGER CAR ONLY) S = SPECIAL TRUCK
H = HEARSE C = CORN-SHELLER/FEED GRINDER W = WELL DRILL A = ANTIQUE N = STORAGE (NORMAL)
L = STORAGE (MILITARY) D = DUPLICATE U = DEALER (UD) T = NON-TRANSFERABLE/NON-NEGOTIABLE
P = PRIVATE SCHOOL BUS.

NOTICE OF ASSIGNMENT OF CERTIFICATE OF TITLE

The undersigned hereby gives notice that he has this day assigned the certificate of title to the vehicle described on the reverse side to:

_____   BUYER _____
            DATE   ADDRESS _____

                                  SELLER _____

NOTICE OF ASSIGNMENT OF CERTIFICATE OF TITLE BY IOWA LICENSED DEALER

The undersigned licensed dealer hereby gives notice that he has this day reassigned the certificate of title to the vehicle described on the reverse hereof to:

_____   BUYER _____
            DATE   ADDRESS _____

_____   DEALER _____
   IA DEALERS LIC NO.
                                  BY _____

CAUTION: This is a notice only and does not in any manner transfer title or ownership to the vehicle described.

The registration shows ownership of a vehicle and in which state it is registered. Left in the car, it is an invitation to steal.

vehicle is sold. When the seller purchases another vehicle of like status (car, truck, or camper), the plates are re-registered and placed on the newly purchased vehicle.

Motorcycles are titled in the same manner in which automobiles and trucks are titled.

Camping and travel trailers, boats, and boat trailers are titled in the same manner in title states which require them to be titled. Some title states do not require nonmotorized vehicles such as camping and travel trailers, boats, and boat trailers to be titled. In these states, these vehicles are registered, not titled, in the same manner as vehicles in nontitle states.

Nontitle States

The procedure for securing registration for vehicles in nontitle states is very different from that in title states. When the vehicle is purchased new from the dealership, the purchaser takes the notarized bill of sale and bill of origin to the office of the Department of Motor Vehicles. The clerk runs a check through NCIC and, if the numbers come back clean, registration papers and license plates are issued for that vehicle.

Registration papers show the name and address of the person to whom the vehicle is registered, VIN, license plate number, description of the vehicle, and date of registration. It does not include the name of the lien holder.

There is absolutely no protection for lien holders in nontitle states, since there is nothing to keep the owner from selling the vehicle before it is paid for. Neither is there a way for anyone buying a vehicle to know if a lien is outstanding against that vehicle. There is also no way the buyer can tell if the vehicle has been stolen and made to appear legitimate through changeover.

One big problem with theft in nontitle states are instances when thieves steal autos and trucks from parking areas such as airports and commuter train stations where they are not likely to be missed for some time. They quickly produce several pieces of identification in the name of the person whose name appears on the vehicle's registration papers, then drive to an unsuspecting auto or truck dealership and sell the vehicle as if they were its rightful owner. When the dealer calls the state registration office and has the serial numbers run through NCIC, they come up clean since the vehicle has not yet been reported stolen.

There is also a problem with rental cars in these nontitle states. A thief will rent a late-model auto from one of the better known agencies for a few days or a week, using a phony name. He then takes the rental agreement with the agency letterhead and symbol at the top, places a blank bill of sale just under the letterhead so that it covers the rental information, and runs it through a good copy machine. The result will be a bill of sale on the rental agency letterhead.

This official-looking bill of sale is then filled out as if the vehicle had been sold to the thief by the rental agency. The transaction doesn't draw suspicion since the sale of rental vehicles by the agencies is a well-known annual or biannual event. The thief then takes the bill of sale to the state registration office and has the ownership of the vehicle changed into whatever name he is using. Since the rental agency is not aware of the thief's actions and therefore has not reported the vehicle stolen, the check through NCIC will not reveal the theft.

Once the thief has named himself as the new owner on the registration papers, he has the amount of time remaining on the rental agreement to sell the vehicle.

Car license plates are a dead giveaway that something is amiss if they don't match the car registration. Less obvious clues that a car may be stolen are rust spots on the license from washers that have been removed, or indentations from different-size washers than those presently installed.

There have been cases in nontitle states of persons with false identities establishing a credit rating, putting a minimum down payment on a ten-thousand-dollar vehicle, financing the balance, then selling the vehicle and skipping town before the first payment comes due.

The notary public is the only safeguard nontitle states have to establish the validity of a sale. This creates a sense of false security since people assume the notary was satisfied with the identities of the parties and the legality of the vehicle. The truth is most notaries will witness, sign, and place their seal on almost anything with no questions asked, especially if they are given five dollars for their trouble. Notary seals are also far too easy to steal and purchase to make them effective security.

Vehicles stolen in nontitle states are most likely to be sold in nontitle states. The reason? Before a vehicle from a nontitle state can be sold in a title state, a title must be secured for that vehicle. Officials in title states are very cautious when dealing with vehicles from nontitle states. Several title states require all vehicles from nontitle states to undergo a thorough examination and background investigation by the local police department and impose a thirty-day waiting period before a title is granted. This policy serves to effectively deter thieves who are looking for a fast buck.

Salvage Laws

Salvage laws are designed to prevent unsafe and stolen vehicles, mainly autos and trucks, from being placed on the highways. Unfortunately, very few states presently have salvage laws. States that do have them, have written and enforced them so weakly that they actually encourage what they were intended to deter.

When a vehicle is declared a total wreck in the states with the best salvage laws, it cannot under any circumstances be placed back into service. The VIN plate is removed and the title is surrendered to the Department of Motor Vehicles and destroyed. When enforced in this manner, this law *is* effective.

However, under the exact same law there is a loophole. Vehicles are declared total wrecks by insurance companies and agencies, not the state transportation department. So if a private individual without insurance does not report his totally damaged vehicle to the transportation department, he can sell the vehicle to another person complete with title (once it has been cleared of all liens) and registration. Or, he can have the vehicle repaired and sell it without the buyer ever knowing the vehicle was once totally wrecked.

On the other hand, the person who bought the vehicle in its totally wrecked condition could repair it for sale, or, if he's a thief, use the title, registration papers, license plates, and VIN plate to convert a stolen vehicle into a legitimate one.

Another kind of salvage law is one that requires the titles of totally wrecked vehicles to be stamped *salvage.* Theoretically, this will notify all future owners that the vehicle was once so severely damaged it had been considered no more than salvage.

The law requiring the title to be stamped *salvage* not only presents a problem of enforcement, it leaves another loophole as well. If the new owner wants a title for the vehicle that does not show that it was severely damaged, he can merely go to the title office, tell the clerk he lost his title and apply for a new one. After the customary check through NCIC, and a check of state title records to assure there is no lien outstanding against the title, a new, unstamped title is issued. There is no way for future owners to know the vehicle was once salvage.

Another kind of salvage law is one that requires salvage yard operators to surrender the VIN plates of totally wrecked vehicles. If the vehicle is purchased by a rebuilder for restoration, he must produce an invoice for each part used to replace a damaged one and undergo an examination by a police agency to insure he is not using stolen parts before a new VIN plate is issued.

Some states that permit rebuilding of salvaged vehicles require the rebuilders to be licensed by the state and have no prior criminal record.

The problem with salvage laws that permit vehicle rebuilding lies in identifying the parts used for rebuilding. Ninety-nine percent of all auto parts have no serial numbers which can be checked. If the rebuilder possesses an invoice from Joe's Junk Yard for all the parts used to rebuild a certain vehicle, and Joe says he sold him the parts, there is no way the police can prove he did not.

One solution to this problem would be to require rebuilders to repair vehicles with new parts. The new parts would have to be purchased from established parts houses and dealerships, which are less likely to be involved in invoice selling. If police would check out all invoices to make sure the parts listed were actually purchased from the dealer, the system would be practically foolproof.

Nontitle states do not have salvage laws because they would be meaningless and because rebuilders rarely purchase wrecked vehicles for use in stolen vehicle conversions. Thieves know they can get legitimate papers for unwrecked vehicles that are stolen, as easily as they can for wrecked vehicles that are not stolen.

Title states without salvage laws unwittingly encourage auto theft. States where there is absolutely no restriction on, and no enforcement of, buying, selling, rebuilding, and reselling wrecked vehicles become havens for conversion thieves. As you will see in the next chapter, any thief can transform a totally wrecked vehicle into what appears to be legitimate transportation in one afternoon for under six hundred dollars. This vehicle can then be kept for personal use without fear of apprehension or sold on the retail market.

Salvage laws are seldom applicable to camping and travel trailers, motorcycles, boats, and airplanes. Camping and travel trailers are rarely involved in accidents and can roll down a mountain and still be repaired more cheaply than they can be replaced.

Motorcycles must be completely destroyed in order to be declared salvage and even then they will not be found in salvage yards.

Boats are not affected by salvage laws. Although there are several ways to convert a salvage boat, papers are so easy to obtain for any kind of a boat that a thief will usually not go through the salvage method.

Airplanes are not subject to any state laws related to title and salvage. The FAA governs all rules and regulations pertaining to aircraft.

3 Changeover Mistakes

Many mistakes due to carelessness and ignorance of technique can be made by the changeover artist during a conversion. Since a thief usually learns his trade from other thieves, he may be given the wrong information by someone who does not know the proper technique himself. The mistakes are passed on from the teacher to the student and eventually end up on the vehicle.

Many of these mistakes are by no means insignificant, though they may appear to be. Even the most trivial error can alert police to investigate further or make an arrest. An observant, knowledgeable citizen can save both inconvenience and money by looking for suspect, telltale signs.

Serial Numbers

Regardless of the vehicle or the method used to convert it, changing the VIN or plate is the most critical part of the entire operation. It is here most mistakes lie.

When a VIN plate is taken from a salvaged auto and placed on another auto, the color of that plate must be the exact color as the plate removed from the stolen auto. Mismatched color is readily apparent upon close examination. If the plate is mounted on top of the dashboard, the edges of the plate may show signs of another color. Often the thief will spray paint the top of the plate and miss the edges.

Look for brush strokes in the paint of the VIN plate. There should be none since the plates are originally spray painted, not brush painted.

A thief who is not too alert may install the VIN plate backward so the numbers face the interior of the auto. The numbers should always face outward. Look for a plate that is installed crookedly. If the rivet holes do not match exactly, the thief will have to redrill the holes. If the holes are not drilled correctly, the plate may be crooked.

If the plate is installed on top of the dashboard, look for slight damage around the rivets. When removing the plate the thief may have ground off the rivets from the top instead of the bottom and touched the plate with the grinding wheel in the process.

If the rivets are exposed, look for loose, undersized, oversized, or the wrong kind of rivets.

If the plate is located on top of the dashboard, look around the edge of the plate for an indentation larger than the plate itself. A VIN plate often leaves an indentation or impression. If a new plate is installed, it may not cover completely the old impression.

A thief may use tape that is too narrow when he is changing the VIN by placing a new number made from a label maker over the old one. Look closely for an exposed edge along each side of the numbers. The opening in the dashboard through which the VIN is viewed is three-eighths to one-half inch wide. In a professional duplication, the label tape will be at least this wide so there are no exposed edges.

If label tape is not glued in place with a firm adhesive, it may loosen when it becomes hot. Look for any bow in the numbers. If the tape is not put on correctly, the numbers will be crooked.

If the thief does not put enough pressure on the handles of the label-making machine when he is making new numbers, they will not be fully embossed, or will be unevenly embossed. Look for uneven numbers.

When examining VIN plates on the driver's door of trucks, look for signs of damage around the rivets. Since all of the plate is exposed, the thief may remove it from the front instead of the back. If it is removed in this manner, the plate is easily damaged and difficult to repair.

Look around the edge of the plate for an impression in the paint where an old plate was removed and which the new plate did not cover.

The rivets on the VIN plate of trucks should look as tarnished and old as the plate. When a vehicle is converted, new rivets are usually installed which will appear bright against the old plate.

On camping and travel trailers and motorcycles, there is no plate, but the VIN numbers may have been altered. An uneven surface in the area of the numbers is a sure sign the numbers were ground off.

A too-smooth surface where the serial numbers are located is also a dead giveaway of alteration. A thief may grind off or weld the numbers and not redress the surface to its original texture. Grind marks may also be visible.

It is difficult for an amateur to restamp numbers as expertly as the manufacturer stamps numbers. Look for numbers that are out of line with the other numbers or at an uneven depth.

Fresh paint is also cause for further inspection. The

paint of the entire frame and tongue should appear the same age. If only the tongue of a trailer, or a small part of the motorcycle's frame appears to be freshly painted, it could be a changeover job.

Look closely at the bow of a boat to see if there is a sign of previous numbers being removed. This should never be the case since numbers are assigned for the life of the boat. If the boat has an identification plate, notice the edges to see if there was a larger previous plate. Look for damage around the rivets that secure the plate.

License Plates

Most people think that when a license plate is removed from one vehicle and placed on another, it looks identical. This is not always true.

Washers are usually used to install a license plate, and, in time, will rust and leave impressions. When a plate is removed from one vehicle and placed on another, rust rings will be visible on the license plate if smaller washers or no washers are used when reinstalling the plate. In states where the license plate remains with the vehicle when it is sold, rust rings should be a sure sign for suspicion.

Service Stickers

Service stickers, those little tags the man at the service station pastes on the door when an auto or truck is serviced, can be great giveaways. Very few thieves will ever think of removing old service stickers when converting a vehicle. Since many of these stickers list the license number or VIN of the vehicle, they can be compared to the numbers on that vehicle. If the numbers of the VIN plate appear on the sticker, and the numbers of the plate on the dashboard or door do not match, either the serviceman made a mistake when he filled out the sticker, or the vehicle is a changeover.

If a policeman is in doubt about the legitimacy of a vehicle, he can look at the service sticker, check the date of service, and ask the driver when the vehicle was last serviced. If he does not know, there is reason for suspicion.

Inspection Stickers

The VIN number or license plate number is listed on the back of the safety inspection sticker. A thief will often neglect to remove an old sticker and install a new one, so this is an important point to check. If it was not necessary for the thief to change the sticker, such as when the steal-strip-purchase-repair method is used, he may be asked the location of the inspection station which issued the sticker. If it is his vehicle, he should know.

Painting

Very few stolen vehicles are repainted, but a few amateurs still make this careless mistake. It is an easy one to spot. To detect a hot paint job, open the hood and trunk and compare the outer color with the inner color. Seldom does a spray painter go to the trouble of painting the inside of the trunk and under the hood so the colors match. Even if these areas are painted, look for crepey, orange-peel ripples in the paint. This is due to improper sanding of the areas before painting.

Also look for overspray on trunk mats and engine parts, especially around the firewall. To avoid overspray, some thieves use brushes to paint these areas, so look for brush marks as well. Spray guns don't leave brush marks.

Engine, Transmission, and Frame Numbers

The engine, transmission, and frame numbers are often the clinchers in stolen vehicle cases. These should be the first numbers checked when a vehicle is suspect. A thief will often change the engine block and transmission case, but neglect to change the frame number, so check it closely. In most states, possession of a vehicle with altered numbers carries the same penalty under the law as possessing a stolen vehicle, so it really is a waste of time to change them.

Registration Papers

There are few mistakes a thief can make with legitimate registration papers even though the vehicle is stolen. Converting a vehicle that does not exactly match the registration papers is the one frequently made mistake that, though it seems rather stupid, does happen.

If the registration lists the vehicle as a 1980 Ford LTD, four-door sedan, the careless thief might steal a 1980 Ford LTD, four-door hardtop. Or if he has the registration for a twenty-one-foot Holiday Travel Trailer, he might steal a twenty-foot Holiday Travel Trailer and never know the difference.

The actual length of a truck wheelbase is very difficult to guess from a cursory glance. The thief might steal a truck identical to that listed on the registration, but with a wheelbase a couple inches shorter or longer. It is sheer guesswork to distinguish a sixteen-and-a-half-foot boat from a seventeen-footer of the same make.

Anyone examining the registration papers and title of a vehicle should closely compare the papers with the vehicle and never assume that they are identical because the person who has the papers says so. Besides noticing the obvious discrepancies, a tape measure should be used to definitely determine if the sizes are correct.

4 Hot Car For Sale

There are as many ways to sell stolen and converted vehicles as there are to change them over. Usually the means used to sell the vehicle have a lot to do with the method used to convert it. For example, a duplicated vehicle is usually sold immediately after conversion, while a vehicle converted by the salvage yard or steal-strip-purchase-repair methods may be sold at leisure since it is less likely to be quickly detected.

Selling To Dealerships

Very few converted vehicles are sold to dealerships. Most thieves think a dealer will check more thoroughly into the ownership of a vehicle before purchasing it. They also know they will receive the lowest offer from a dealer. However, when it comes to making a fast buck, a not-too-sharp dealer is just the person to sell to.

When selling his car to a dealer, the thief acts just like any person trying to get top dollar for his vehicle. Since most vehicles are traded on higher-priced models, the thief first asks how much he will be allowed on a trade-in. But because he has no intention of trading,

FOR SALE

Divorce settlement forces sale. 1981 Cadillac
Eldorado Biaritz, fully equipped, low mileage. 1978 Corvette, special edition. Boat and
trailer, Smoker Craft 14-foot, aluminum,
used only one season. 1980 Honda XL500S
motorcycle, low mileage, perfect condition.
Family Airstream travel trailer, 20-foot,
great shape. Priced to sell. Ready to deal.
821 Suburbia Drive, 981-9072, evenings and
weekends.

An ad such as this might be placed in the newspaper by a thief
who wants to turn a big profit in a short time. He may have only
recently rented the home he is selling from. He will have moved
away by the time any of his vehicles are investigated, and left no
forwarding address.

the conversation will eventually result in an outright sale, after the dealer and the thief haggle over the price.

The dealer then calls the state registration or title office to make sure that the vehicle is registered to the person whose name is on the registration and that the title is free of all liens. The license plates and VIN are compared with the registration to make sure all numbers match, and, since they do, the dealer is satisfied the vehicle is the property of the seller.

If the thief is selling the vehicle in the name of the rightful owner and does not have identification bearing that name, he will ask for payment in cash. If the ownership of the vehicle has been changed to the name in which he has identification, he will accept a check since he will have no trouble cashing it.

Once the thief has received payment, he will disappear from the dealership never to return to it. If the sale is made where the thief is not known, has no prior criminal record, and doesn't have his picture on file with the police department, there is practically no chance that he will be identified.

Selling Through Advertisements

Newspaper and other advertisements are the most popular and profitable means of selling converted vehicles. The thief knows that the last thing a person expects when he follows up on an advertisement is a stolen and converted auto. By pricing the vehicle midway between wholesale and retail, the thief is assured of a quick sale.

Before the vehicle can be advertised, the thief must first make some preparations. He will rent a furnished apartment or house at an economic level comparable to that of the vehicle he will sell. For example, if the thief is selling a Cadillac, Lincoln, or Mercedes, he will rent in an affluent neighborhood. If he is selling a Chevy or Ford, he will rent in a middle-class neighborhood.

He will have a telephone installed and listed in the name he will use to sell the vehicle, then place an advertisement in the newspaper. If there is a local vehicle advertisement magazine published, he should also advertise in it.

When a potential buyer calls, he will behave as any person would who is selling a vehicle. If the buyer offers a couple of hundred dollars less than the asking price for the vehicle, the thief will accept the offer. If the offer is too low, he will reject it, or take the name and number of the person in the event he doesn't get a better one.

If an agreement on price is reached, the purchaser must come up with the money. Since 80 percent of all vehicles are financed, the purchaser will take the VIN and license plate number to the lien holder who will make a standard check of registration and title records. Since the vehicle is registered to the person whose name appears on the registration and title papers, the check will come back clean and, providing the prospective purchaser has acceptable credit, a check will be issued for the amount of purchase.

The purchaser will bring the check to the thief who will give the registration, title papers, and car to him. The thief will disappear and the new owner will take the papers to the registration office and have ownership changed to his name. If the conversion has been done properly, the vehicle may change hands several times and never be detected as stolen.

Another twist to the advertisement method of sale is to sell not one, but several vehicles from the same location, even from the *same* advertisement. When I was operating in Indianapolis, Indiana, I once rented a house in a very nice section of town and sold six 1-year-old Eldorado Cadillacs in two days with the same ad by pricing them sixteen hundred dollars below the going price. I parked two Eldorados in the driveway and told people who came to see them that I had to sell one of them. As soon as one was sold, I would replace it with another until all were sold. I have known other thieves who sold as many as eighteen vehicles from the same location before disappearing.

Several different kinds of vehicles can also be sold from the same location. A thief may offer two automobiles, a camper trailer and a boat in the same ad. He will say he is moving out of the country and is selling everything he owns. My partner once sold two automobiles, a pickup truck, a camper trailer, and three 20-foot boats in one weekend from the same location.

Selling At Public Auctions

Public auctions are the most popular places for amateur changeover artists to sell their vehicles. The action is fast and payment is usually in cash, creating a made-to-order situation for thieves.

Many auctions require vehicles to be enrolled and their VIN registrations and titles to be checked and cleared prior to auction time. Since the vehicles are properly registered, even though they are stolen, this poses no real problem for the thief. He simply enrolls his vehicle and lets the auction house run the check.

When his goods have been auctioned off, the thief will accept the highest offer and insist on payment in cash. Since this is not uncommon at auctions, it does not draw suspicion.

A thief may sell several vehicles at the same auction,

such as an automobile, camper trailer, pickup truck, or boat. Or, he may pay someone to sell a vehicle for him under a different name. This keeps the auction operators from becoming suspicious of him.

Selling To Yourself

Sometimes a thief will convert a vehicle he wishes to keep for his personal use. Since he does not want to chance being arrested if the vehicle is discovered to be stolen, he will "sell" the vehicle to himself. It is an easy, inexpensive safeguard against apprehension.

The thief will place an advertisement in the newspaper listing the vehicle he wishes to convert and keep. He will list the phone number of a telephone booth as the number to call. This establishes a party from which the vehicle has been bought.

He will then falsify a bill of sale from the person who previously held the registration to himself as the new owner and have it notarized.

A receipt for the amount of purchase is prepared to show payment was made. The registration and title are then transferred into the name of the thief as the new owner.

The thief knows that if the vehicle is ever detected as a stolen conversion, he can "remember" the newspaper advertisement which attracted him to the vehicle, and produce the receipt and bill of sale from the person he says sold it to him.

The police will check out the phone number which appeared in the advertisement and trace it to the telephone booth. If the thief in possession of the vehicle has no prior criminal record, the police will probably think he bought the vehicle unknowingly, and the investigation will be dropped.

However, if the thief has a previous criminal record of any kind, the police will search for other clues that tie him to the vehicle before the purchase date. If they cannot make this connection, they cannot press charges, although they may suspect that the thief either knowingly purchased it or changed it over himself.

_ _ _ _ _ _ _ _ _ _ _ _ _ _ _ _ _

Auction houses tend to make the sale of converted vehicles far too easy. If they would go the extra mile and check the motor, transmission, and frame numbers, as well as the VIN, most amateur thieves would be stopped. Amateurs do not go to the trouble of changing all numbers, and attend to only those which might be checked. To make a bad situation even worse, some auction houses do not require any kind of check for ownership or legitimacy before a vehicle is sold. This is an open invitation to thieves selling converted vehicles.

5 Private Purchasers, Beware!

A private buyer is the most vulnerable of all prospects when it comes to purchasing a stolen and converted vehicle. Naive and anxious to get a good deal on his dream car or vehicle, his cautiousness may be blunted. Besides, everyone assumes that the vehicle being sold is the legal property of the person whose name appears on the registration and title papers, and that the seller is that person. Obviously, this is not always true.

Suppose, for example, you see an automobile you like in the classified section of the newspaper. You call the number listed and drop by to inspect the vehicle. It appears in excellent condition, has low mileage, all the options you wanted, and the seller has a clear title. The price is about nine hundred dollars less than the comparably equipped cars you have seen. You go to the bank to borrow the money, pay the seller, and register the car in your name.

Three months later the police come to your house to inspect your automobile. They inform you that your car is a changeover, that it has been stolen and duplicated to match a legitimate auto. What do you do? Cry? Probably.

The police will confiscate your automobile and return it to its rightful owner or the insurance company that paid off the claim when it was stolen. You will have to continue making payments on the automobile you no longer have because *you,* not the bank, are responsible for not knowing the vehicle was stolen.

But misery and frustration can be avoided if a buyer will make a few simple inquiries to assure the vehicle and seller are really who they are supposed to be.

First, check out the seller. Ask to see several pieces of identification and compare them to the name and address listed on the registration papers. If the person says he does not have his identification with him or refuses to show it, the transaction should be ended.

If the person rents his house or apartment, ask his landlord how long he has been living in the residence. If he has lived there only a few days or a few weeks, beware.

If the signature of the owner appears on the registration papers, ask the seller to write his name and compare the two signatures.

If you are convinced the owner and the seller are the same person, then check out the vehicle. Don't check one and let the other go without suspicion. Remember, it is very possible for the seller to have what appears to be legitimate identification and still be selling a stolen vehicle.

Since most converted vehicles are second-owned, always call the previous owners and ask the condition of the vehicle when they sold it. If they say they have not sold the vehicle, you are probably looking at a duplicate. If they tell you the last time they saw the vehicle it had a train parked on top of it or was wrapped around a telephone pole, you probably have a salvage yard changeover on your hands. You wouldn't want a vehicle that has been damaged so severely.

If the vehicle passes this test, go down the list of changeover mistakes and look for any telltale errors that disclose the bad news. Pay close attention to the service and inspection stickers. If they are new or if the owner doesn't know when they were put on, something may be wrong.

Look at the dates of the registration papers to see if they were recently registered. If the seller has just bought and registered the vehicle, why would he be selling it?

If the vehicle passes all the above tests, you are ready to put it through its final examination. *Personally* copy the serial numbers from the vehicle's engine block, transmission case, and frame. Take these numbers to the state registration office and ask the clerk to run a check on them through NCIC. If the numbers come back clean, and the vehicle has not been stolen, don't feel foolish. After all, it's your money that could have been lost if you had purchased a stolen vehicle.

All of these rules also apply when you are purchasing a vehicle at a public auction. The time to check out a vehicle at an auction is *before* it goes on the block. Afterward there will not be enough time. Go early and don't be so anxious to get a good deal that you leave your logic behind.

I cannot overemphasize the need for inquiry by a private individual interested in buying any vehicle. Nothing should be assumed! Do not omit a single part of the checklist. If you do, you may miss the one thing which will tell you the vehicle is stolen.

It is true that no matter how closely some converted vehicles are checked, the changeover will not be detectable. But these cases are very rare and the conversion professionally done. If you do get one of these vehicles, neither you, nor the next owner, nor anyone else is ever going to know that this vehicle has been converted.

6 Auto Conversion

Of the estimated one million automobiles stolen in the United States each year, only about 10 percent are converted into seemingly legitimate transportation for permanent personal use or sale. The only surprise about this figure is that it is not higher. State laws and police enforcement are so lax that the percentage could easily double if more thieves understood the loopholes in the present laws. Fortunately, most thieves are uneducated and too lazy to familiarize themselves with the laws they break.

The Salvage Yard Method

The easiest, safest, and most popular method of automobile conversion is the use of legitimate papers from totally wrecked vehicles. It is easy because the VIN plate, title, and registration of wrecked automobiles are readily available. It is safe because detection of a vehicle that was once stolen is unlikely if the conversion is done so well that the buyer or a policeman does not suspect foul play and go beyond the standard checks.

Regardless of whether this kind of conversion is made in a title or nontitle state, the procedure is the same, except that in a title state the thief must also change the ownership on the title to the name he is using.

In almost 100 percent of all auto conversion cases, the automobile will be a slightly used vehicle, not a new, previously unregistered one. This means the thief must first change the VIN plate from the wrecked auto to the stolen auto so it will not appear on the stolen roster when a check is run through NCIC. Secondly, he must produce the previous registration and title papers of the wrecked vehicle if the converted auto is to be reregistered in another name or sold.

In the following step-by-step look at the salvage method, we will assume that the state in which the operation is taking place does not have salvage laws governing the sale of totally wrecked autos, unless otherwise specified.

The first thing the thief must do is check salvage yards for a totally wrecked auto of the make and model he wishes to convert. When he has located such an auto, he will approach the salvage operator and ask to purchase it, telling him that he wants the auto for rebuilding purposes, or to make into a race car.

Since the thief is only interested in the VIN plate and title and registration papers, the vehicle needs to be no more than a hull. There need be no front end, rear end, windows, doors, interior, suspension, wheels, axles or other usable parts which can be sold. As long as the VIN plate is intact and the salvage operator is willing to sell the hull complete with title and registration, even if the title is stamped *salvage*, the thief will gladly purchase it.

If the VIN plate has been removed, or the salvage

operator will not release the title and registration papers with the vehicle, the thief will go elsewhere.

But a salvage operator is usually happy to accommodate these "hull hounds." With all salable parts removed, he can only place it in a crusher and sell it to a metal recycler for fifty dollars. On the other hand, a hull hound will pay up to six hundred dollars for the same piece of junk.

After purchasing the hull, the thief will take it to a garage or his home workshop and remove the VIN plate listing the serial numbers for the auto, which correspond to numbers on its title and registration papers. The VIN plate is located on the driver's side of the dashboard about six inches from the windshield post and one inch back from the windshield. The location is the same on every American and foreign-made automobile, pickup truck, and small van sold in the United States.

Until 1968 the VIN plate was located on the driver's door. But a U.S. Supreme Court decision in 1967 stated that when a police officer opened the door of a vehicle without benefit of a search warrant and checked the VIN plate to see if the vehicle was stolen, he violated the suspect's rights guaranteed by the U.S. Constitution to be free from illegal search and seizure. The plate was then removed from the door and placed on the dashboard where police can see the serial numbers without actually entering the vehicle.

The VIN plate is affixed to the dashboard with two rivets. On some vehicles, these rivets are exposed; on others, they are unexposed. The kind of rivet used also varies with the kind of vehicle. For example, General Motors uses round rivets, while Ford Motor Company uses hexagon-headed rivets.

The VIN plate can also be mounted under the dashboard. When mounted underneath, there will be a one-

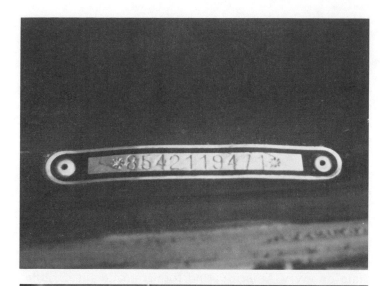

The VIN plates on autos are attached to the dash as a top-mount (top) or under-dash mount (bottom). When changing the VIN plate, the thief must take care to match color, rivet size and head configuration, and plate size to avoid arousing suspicion.

half by three-inch hole in the dashboard through which the serial numbers can be read. On all models, the serial numbers face forward and are read from left to right.

Regardless of the shape of the rivets and where the plate is mounted, the procedure for removal is always the same. The speedometer, tachometer, fuel and oil gauges are removed to give easy access to the bottom side of the plate and rivets. It is not practical to try to reach the plate from underneath the dashboard without removing the gauges due to air-conditioning, vent ducts and wiring.

A small, hand-held hobby grinder can then be used to grind off the bottom heads of the rivets flush with the plate and a screwdriver used to gently pry loose the plate. The thief is always careful not to damage the plate in any way since it will be placed on the auto he plans to steal and convert.

If there are parts on the vehicle that can be sold, the thief will remove and sell them to recover the cost of the hull. The thief will then destroy the remainder of the vehicle by cutting it into small pieces for burial in a landfill or lake, or he will sell or donate the remains to another salvage dealer who will crush and recycle it.

Once the thief is in possession of the VIN plate and corresponding title and registration papers, he must decide if he wants to keep or sell the vehicle he will convert. If he intends to sell the auto and does not think he will need identification to do so, or if he can get identification in the name of the person the vehicle was previously registered to, he will not bother changing the title and registration to another name. The vehicle remains registered in the name of the previous owner since salvage operators are not required to change the ownership of vehicles they intend to dismantle for parts into their own names.

If the thief plans to keep the vehicle for his own use or wants the registration listed in a name for which he has identification, he must have the title and registration changed. This is merely a matter of filling out a bill of sale, having it notarized, and carrying it along with the title and registration papers to the appropriate state office. Since the auto he is reregistering is, in fact, a legitimate auto, and the one he will convert has not yet been stolen, the request will be processed routinely.

If the title is stamped *salvage*, the thief must secure a new, unstamped title as described in the previous chapter before the ownership can be changed.

After the question of whose name the vehicle will be registered in has been resolved and the necessary changes made, if any, the registration papers (pink slip or tag receipt) are taken to the license plate office. Unless the auto came with license plates, new ones are purchased and a new tag receipt issued in the name of the person to whom the vehicle is now registered. If the vehicle had license plates when it was purchased from the salvage dealer, they are retained and a new tag receipt is issued in the name of the new owner.

The thief is then ready to select the vehicle he will steal and convert. Since the vehicle must *exactly* match the vehicle he purchased at the salvage yard as described on the registration papers, this can take a few hours or a few days. Most professional changeover artists will not steal a vehicle within fifty miles of the city where it will be driven or sold so that its rightful owner will not recognize it on the street. They also know that the police do not actively search for a vehicle outside that radius.

When looking for a vehicle to steal, a thief does not necessarily take the first exact match he finds. Since he is not going to be paying extra for the options, he selects the one with the most and best equipment and lowest mileage, and in the best physical condition.

If the color of the vehicle is listed on the title and registration, he must match that color *exactly*. For example, if the color is listed on the registration papers as "D. Blue," this means the vehicle is dark blue. If it is listed as "L. Blue," the color is light blue. A thief cannot use the registration of a light blue vehicle for a dark blue, red, or yellow one. If no color is listed, the thief can choose any color he desires.

It is important to note that the color listed on the registration papers is the *exterior* color only. It has nothing to do with the interior color. Thus a vehicle listed as "D. Blue" may have any color interior.

Once the thief has selected and stolen a vehicle, he immediately takes it to his garage or home for conversion. He will remove and destroy the license plates and replace them with the license plates from the hull he purchased at salvage, or those he purchased for it from the tag office.

The most critical part of the conversion is changing the VIN plate. The plate is removed from the stolen auto just as it was removed from the salvaged vehicle and the VIN plate from the salvaged hull is installed on the stolen vehicle by riveting it in place from the bottom with a pop-rivet gun. The gun can be purchased from any automotive store.

The thief must be certain the rivets used to install the new plate are exactly like those that held the old plate in place. For example, if the rivets are exposed from the top of the dashboard and are hexagonal, they cannot be replaced by round-headed or square-headed rivets. If brass rivets are removed, steel rivets cannot be installed in their place. In shape and material, the new rivets must match the old.

Some states require a safety inspection sticker, others do not. The reverse side of the sticker carries the VIN number of the car and the sticker must be replaced by a thief if all details of a duplicated auto are to match.

The color of the VIN plate is also critical, since it will always exactly match the color of the dashboard. Therefore, a red plate cannot be placed on a blue dashboard, or even on one of a different shade of red. To do so would invite suspicion. This does not mean, however, that the thief must steal an auto with a dashboard the same color as the VIN plate he has. He can buy a can of matching spray paint and recolor the VIN plate before it is installed.

Once the VIN plate has been properly installed, the gauges reinstalled, and the license plates securely attached, only one detail remains before the conversion is complete—the safety inspection sticker. If the vehicle has a safety inspection sticker, the number of the VIN plate will be listed on the back. Since the VIN plate has been changed, the safety sticker must also be changed. It can be removed by wetting it with a warm, damp towel to loosen the adhesive, then scraping it off with a razor blade.

The vehicle can be inspected at a safety inspection station and a new sticker installed which lists the number of the new VIN plate. The conversion is complete; the auto can be driven or sold.

The serial numbers of the motor, transmission, and frame have not been changed, however, and each could lead to the discovery of the vehicle as stolen. These numbers do not appear on the registration papers though, and are not checked by the title and registration office when registration is changed. The thief knows that if he is stopped by the police, they will check his driver's license and vehicle registration papers. Since the VIN serial number and the license plate number appear on the tag receipt, and neither will come up stolen in an NCIC check, law officers will not suspect the vehicle is a changeover. The vehicle will possibly make it through its ten-year vehicle life expectancy without ever being detected.

Chop Shops

Stealing an auto for its parts is equivalent to kidnapping a person and using his or her heart, kidneys, eyes, skin, and other organs in transplant operations. In the changeover industry, such an operation begins at a *chop shop* where perfectly good vehicles are dismantled, or chopped up, and sold to auto body repair shops where they replace damaged parts.

People who buy these parts either don't know, or don't want to know, that they came from a chop shop. For example, if a body shop operator needs to repair a new Ford Thunderbird with the entire front end damaged, he must buy replacement parts. If he purchases these parts new from a Ford dealership, they may cost as much as twenty-five hundred dollars. If he buys the parts used from one of the local salvage yards, they may cost eighteen hundred dollars. But he can buy the same parts from a little garage across town for nine hundred dollars. Which do you think he will buy the parts from? The little garage across town, of course.

Although he may suspect that the parts came from a chop shop, he dares not ask, nor does he *want* to know. As long as no one tells him, he doesn't care whether they came from a wrecked car or a stolen one.

Many chop shops take orders from body shop operators. The operator will call the chop shop with a list of the parts he needs to repair a certain car. The chop shop manager will always say he has the parts in stock, although he probably doesn't at the time the order is received. After all, the streets are full of "parts" and it's a simple matter to send someone out to pick up what is needed.

When the manager of the chop shop gets an order, he will dispatch a thief to locate and steal a vehicle bearing the necessary parts. The vehicle is pulled into a garage or warehouse where four men will go to work removing all salable parts. The parts needed to fill the orders are removed first and shipped to the body shop that placed the order. Other parts are sold to salvage yards, whose operators may or may not be aware of the operation, and other businesses such as glass companies, upholstery repair shops, tire dealers, parts houses, rebuilders who will resell the parts as rebuilt ones, and engine and transmission shops.

Seldom are these parts used to rebuild an auto bought at a salvage yard. There are too many other ways which require much less work to convert salvage autos into seemingly legitimate transportation. Only an amateur or a private individual would bother.

_ _ _ _ _ _ _ _ _ _ _ _ _ _ _ _ _

Whenever a vehicle is stolen, the theft affects the party from which it was stolen, the insurance companies, and if it is detected, the person who bought it after it was converted. But when vehicles are stolen and run through chop shops, the harm is far greater. Chop shops tend to reach out and corrupt other elements of society. Businessmen who would otherwise not violate the law are drawn into the web by the high profits. Dealing with a chop shop can easily double net profits.

As long as car manufacturers continue to construct vehicles with parts that do not have numbers, they will be stolen and dismantled. Imprinting manufacturers' serial numbers on all parts *could* put a damper on the chop shop business, but *only* if there were some means of enforcement. One simple solution to the enforcement problem is to reinspect wrecked vehicles before they are placed back into service. A check of NCIC could be made of all numbers. Unfortunately, auto industry lobbyists who oppose the numbering of all parts still prevent this from becoming a reality.

7 Auto Duplicating

A little-known segment of the changeover industry is *automotive duplicating*, the art of taking stolen automobiles and converting them for short-term use or sale by duplicating the registration papers and VIN plates of identical automobiles that are not stolen. Although this practice is more common in nontitle states, duplicating is possible in title states as well.

Duplicating In Nontitle States

The first step in duplicating is to decide what kind of automobile is wanted for use or sale. For example, if a thief wants a 1982 Ford Thunderbird, a popular and easy-to-sell auto, he will scout parking lots and apartment complexes until he finds a 1982 Thunderbird of the color he wishes to duplicate. He will enter the auto and search the glove compartment and behind the sun visor for the vehicle's registration papers. If he finds the papers, he moves to the next step. Otherwise he keeps looking until he finds the car he wants with the registration papers intact.

With the registration papers in hand, the thief goes

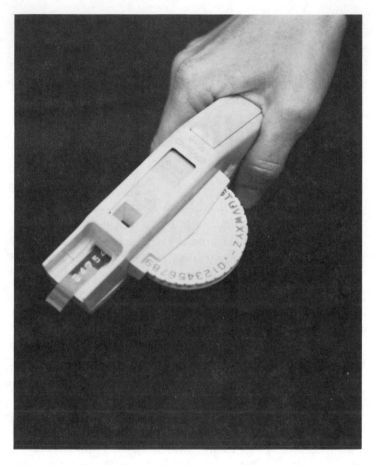

A label-making machine can be used to alter dash-mounted VIN plates. By using good adhesive and the proper-size tape, the thief will fool most persons, unless other discrepancies lead to investigation.

to the state vehicle registration office and reports his license plates lost. The clerk will keep the registration papers stolen from the Thunderbird, fill out new registration papers, and issue new license plates for that vehicle. The thief then has registration papers with matching license plates.

If he intends to register the vehicle in another name, the thief draws up a bill of sale listing the person whose name appears on the registration papers as the seller, and whomever he wishes as the purchaser. After the bill of sale has been notarized, he returns to the state registration office with it and registers the car in the name of the purchaser listed on the bill of sale. The clerk at the registration office will make a check through NCIC to insure that the vehicle has not been stolen. Since only the papers have been stolen, not the vehicle, it will come back clean.

With the license plate and registration conversion complete, the thief is ready to procure the vehicle for duplication. The auto is carefully chosen as described in the previous chapter, stolen, and taken to a garage or to his home for final transformation. The license plates of the stolen auto are removed and the newly acquired license plates are installed. The safety inspection sticker is removed and the glass cleaned in preparation for the new sticker.

He is ready then for the final and critical step of the duplicating process: duplicating the VIN plate. There are two ways this can be done. The best, but most difficult, is to remove the VIN plate from the stolen vehicle and manufacture a new plate bearing the serial number of the vehicle from which the registration papers were stolen. The new VIN plate numbers will match those on the registration papers.

Manufacturing a new VIN plate requires knowledge

of metals and stamping since the numbers are embossed in the plate and not merely stamped on it. There is a shortage of machinery that can produce a quality plate from metal.

Some thieves who make a career of duplicating do have machinery, but others have begun making the plates from plastic. A piece of thin, hard plastic the same size as the VIN plate is placed on a hard piece of rubber, and heated with an electric, forced-air heater until the plastic is soft. The desired serial number is then stamped from right to left with backward stamps.

The hard rubber will cause the plastic to emboss, so that when the plastic plate is turned over, the serial numbers read from left to right. The rivet holes are then aligned and drilled, the plate is painted the exact color of the dashboard and installed.

I once used another, easier method that worked just as well and is much faster. In cases where the VIN plate is mounted underneath the dashboard and must be viewed through an opening, as most are nowadays, I would not manufacture a new plate, but put a new number over the old one. I accomplished this by first removing the VIN plate. Then, using a hand-held label-making machine, which is a low-cost, common apparatus, I stamped out the serial number shown on the registration papers, and glued it over the old number. I reinstalled the plate and the conversion was complete.

I preferred the label-making-machine method because it always produced perfectly lined, evenly embossed numbers identical to those which appear on the original plate. If the label is secured by a super adhesive, it will remain in place forever. Although most label material used in these machines has its own adhesive backing, it tends to come loose when it gets hot from the sun shining through the windshield.

If a thief in a nontitle state does not wish to have the vehicle registered in a new name, and feels safe driving or selling the vehicle while it is still registered in the name of the rightful owner, he need only take the registration papers to the state registration office and report that he has lost his license plates. New plates will be issued, after which he steals the matching auto, changes the serial number on the VIN plate to match the registration papers, removes the safety inspection sticker and installs a new one, and replaces the old license plates with the new ones.

This kind of duplicating usually occurs when the thief wants to make a quick sale to an unsuspecting buyer. In this case, the thief will have identification in the name of the person to whom the vehicle is registered.

Duplicating In Title States

There are two kinds of duplicating in title states. The simplest duplicating involves stealing the registration papers from an automobile exactly like the thief wishes to duplicate. The thief then takes the registration papers to the state registration office and reports his license plates stolen. The clerk will run a stolen check through NCIC and issue new license plates.

The thief then steals a matching auto, removes the old license plates and safety inspection sticker, and replaces them with the newly issued plates and a new safety sticker, and puts the VIN from the registration papers on the VIN plate. With only the registration papers, the thief cannot change the ownership of the vehicle in a title state. The vehicle can be used as if it were the actual vehicle listed on the registration papers, but not sold, since the thief does not have possession of the title.

The second method of duplicating an auto in title states is to secure the title for the vehicle the thief wishes to duplicate. This is strictly a guessing game unless the owner is foolish enough to leave the title in the vehicle. Usually the thief will look in the glove compartments and behind the sun visors of several dozen automobiles, collecting the registration papers from each. If the title of the vehicle is also present, he will, of course, take that.

The thief then calls the state title office and asks for a title check of each of the vehicles. This process may take several days to avoid drawing suspicion by inquiring about several vehicles at one time. If any of the vehicles are owned free and clear and therefore without liens, the thief will set the registration papers for them aside. Registrations for others will be destroyed.

The thief takes the registration papers from one of the vehicles with a clear title to the state title office. He tells the clerk that the title to the vehicle has been lost and asks for a new title. The clerk will check the title records and find that the vehicle has a clear title. The clerk will run a stolen check through NCIC to make sure the automobile has not been stolen, then issue a clear title in the name of the person whose name appears on the registration papers.

With the title and registration papers in his possession, the thief can sell the automobile as if he were the owner listed on the title. Or, he can make out a bill of sale, have it notarized, and have the vehicle's ownership changed into any name he wishes, just as if it were sold by the rightful owner.

Once the title and registration have been changed into a new name, the thief will steal and changeover the automobile as described earlier. The vehicle can be sold in that name.

Duplicating Nontitled Automobiles
In Title States

A vehicle from a nontitle state can be only registered and titled in title states that do not require the inspection of vehicles from nontitle states. When bringing a vehicle into a title state, the thief will steal the registration papers of a vehicle he intends to duplicate and carry them to the title office in a title state that does not require inspection. He will tell the clerk he has recently moved to that state and wants to have his automobile titled and registered. This is a common request and will be processed routinely. There will be the customary NCIC check which will show the vehicle is not stolen. A check of the state in which the vehicle is registered will show the vehicle is registered to the person whose name appears on the registration papers.

Usually the title is issued without delay and the new address within the title state is placed on the title and registration. Some states mail the title to the new address, others require a waiting period before mailing or issuing a title. Once the thief receives the title and registration papers, he can purchase license plates and go about stealing and changing over the vehicle by duplicating.

Duplicating, whether in titled or nontitled states, is always a short-term business. The thief is either trying to secure seemingly legitimate transportation for a month or two, or goods for sale to an unsuspecting buyer. The latter is more common. He realizes that

sooner or later the duplicated vehicle will be sold or
traded and the owner will learn that the vehicle is no
longer registered in his name. This is extremely confus-
ing to both the owner and the police. Since the owner
of the duplicated vehicle is still in possession of the
vehicle, no one can seem to understand why the registration was changed, why new license plates were issued,
and where the vehicle came from that was registered in
its place. Eventually the stolen vehicle will be traced and
confiscated. But this will usually take weeks, even
months, and the thief will be long gone, the money
from the sale will be spent, and another duplicating pro-
ject will be underway.

— — — — — — — — — — — — — — — — — —

Auto duplicating is probably the most difficult kind
of changeover to detect and prevent with present laws.
However, if all states would require that all vehicles be
inspected and *all* of their numbers be checked through
NCIC before they are allowed to be licensed, registered,
and titled, auto duplicating would be stopped entirely.

8 Steal-Strip-Purchase-Repair

Stripping autos for their parts is an old and common practice. Usually the parts are sold and used to repair other damaged vehicles of identical make, model, and year. But the *steal-strip-purchase-repair method* adds a new twist to an old game since, instead of using the stripped parts to repair another vehicle, they are used to repair the vehicle from which they were removed.

Sometimes a thief cannot or does not wish to purchase a totally wrecked auto of the type he wishes to convert. Or he may not feel secure with the duplicating method. High-priced, low-production cars such as the Cadillac Fleetwood Brougham, Lincoln Continental Mark VI, Mercedes 300 SD Turbo Diesel and 450 SL, Jaguar XJS, Ferrari 308 GTS, and Porsche Turbo Carrera and 928 will bring between eighteen and forty-six thousand dollars on the retail market and are very attractive prospects for the thief. They also bring certain challenges to the art of thievery.

For one thing, expensive autos are subject to closer scrutiny by police and potential buyers. For another, drivers of elite automobiles are usually more careful in their driving habits than the average driver, have fewer

This late-model pickup truck rests in a salvage yard, stripped of most usable parts, while the auto is still a parts donor to others like it. A thief can buy them for very little money and rebuild them with parts he previously pilfered or can get on the street. With the legitimate titles in hand, he can sell them without being discovered.

accidents, and contribute fewer totally wrecked automobiles to the salvage yards. Due to the high cost of replacing exotic autos, they are likely to be repaired after
an accident unless they are completely demolished or
stripped of every usable part. The steal-strip-purchase-
repair method affords the thief an opportunity to obtain cars he may be otherwise unable to get.

First, the thief targets an automobile he thinks he
can easily sell, such as a Mercedes 450 SL, steals it, and
carries it to a garage where it is stripped of *all* parts.
I am not talking about just the engine, transmission,
and bucket seats, but every part on the vehicle including
back and front windshields, doors, complete front
and rear ends, doors, brakes, suspension system, wheels,
interior, and gauges. Literally every part worth a dollar
or more is removed. The remainder will be merely a hull
of an auto, worth almost nothing and cheaper to replace
than rebuild. The hull is then taken to an isolated area
and dumped.

To make absolutely certain the hull is found without too much delay, the thief makes an anonymous call
to the police, telling them he saw someone unloading
the hull of an auto in an isolated area and directing
them to the location. The police will, of course, find the
hull, call a wrecker, have it towed to the salvage yard,
and notify the owner, who will notify his insurance
company. The insurance company will send out a claims
adjuster to survey the hull and estimate the cost of
repair. Since the cost of repair would be greater than the
cost of replacement, the claims adjuster will recommend
that the hull of the auto be sold as salvage and a replacement purchased for the owner.

Insurance companies sell all of their totally wrecked
vehicles at salvage pools. A *salvage pool* is an auction
for damaged merchandise held weekly, biweekly, or

monthly, and attended only by licensed salvage dealers. However, there is nothing to prevent a private individual from asking a salvage dealer to go to a salvage pool and buy a certain vehicle for him. When merchandise and vehicles are auctioned at salvage pools, they are sold to the highest bidder. Bids may be sealed or verbal, depending on the policy of the pool.

When the thief's auto hull reaches the salvage pool, he will pay a salvage dealer from fifty to one hundred dollars' commission to bid on the vehicle. Since the hull is of great value to him and of little value to anyone else, he will make sure his bid is high enough to outbid anyone else who might be interested in the auto.

Once the vehicle has been purchased and the title and registration secured, the thief is ready to start rebuilding the hull.

Since the serial numbers of the engine and transmission of the stripped vehicle have been placed on the stolen list with NCIC, the engine block and transmission case must be replaced with new ones. This eliminates the chance of any part of the vehicle ever being on the stolen list. The vehicle is then ready for total restoration using the same parts that were removed earlier, except for the engine block and transmission case.

Once this automobile has been rebuilt, it is absolutely impossible for anyone to ever prove it is a stolen vehicle. The vehicle is the one purchased at the salvage pool but the engine and transmisison do not bear the serial numbers of those which were stolen. If the thief produces false bills of sale for the parts he rebuilt the auto with, and the bills of sale cannot be proven false, he has even greater assurance against apprehension.

No one would suspect that this car was totally stripped, abandoned for police to find, bought as salvage, and then restored with parts a thief previously stripped from it. If the thief properly attended to the paperwork, chances are this changeover will go undiscovered.

It is important to note that the steal-strip-purchase-rebuild method can only be practiced in states with lenient salvage laws, which most have. If the title and salvage laws were written as I stated earlier, this method would be impossible.

9 Tractor-Trailer Conversion

In recent years inflation has pushed the average price of a fully equipped tractor-trailer truck beyond sixty thousand dollars making heavy-duty truck conversion a growing segment of the changeover industry. Since it's not much more trouble to convert a truck than it is to convert an auto, and since the profit margin is five to ten times greater, some thieves are abandoning auto conversion altogether in favor of heavy-duty trucks.

The Salvage Method

When a heavy-duty truck is declared a total wreck by an insurance company, it falls under the same salvage laws as do totally wrecked automobiles. The conversion process is similar to that for autos: using legitimate papers from a totally wrecked truck to make a stolen one appear legal.

Say, for example, a hull hound is prowling through a salvage yard and comes upon a 1979 Freightliner cab-over with tandem axles and a sleeper. The truck hit a bridge abutment about twenty miles an hour over the double-nickel speed limit and the steering wheel was

73

driven against the back wall of the sleeper. The cab has been tilted forward and the engine, transmission, tandem axles, fifth wheel, and all other usable parts have been removed leaving only the wrecked hull of the cab and frame.

The hull hound will purchase the wreck, receive the title and registration papers from the yard operator, and tow the remains to a garage for conversion.

The first thing the thief will do is remove the VIN plate from the truck. This procedure is somewhat different from removing the VIN plate from automobiles. The VIN plate on a heavy-duty truck is on the driver's door, not on the dashboard. Legislation that forced moving the VIN plate from the door of an automobile to the dashboard did not include trucks in the decree, mainly because a policeman cannot stand on the ground and see the dashboard of a truck through the windshield.

To remove the VIN plate from the door, the thief must remove the inside door panel and use a hobby grinder to grind off the back heads of the rivets. This keeps the face of the plate from being damaged. Once the rivets are ground off, the plate is carefully pried loose with a screwdriver or putty knife.

If there are any parts on the wreck that can be salvaged and used or sold, they are removed. The remainder of the wreck is then destroyed, sold, or given to a salvage dealer to be crushed and sent to a metal recycler.

The thief then takes the title and registration to the state title or registration office and changes the ownership into the name he plans to use to sell the truck. After a NCIC check of the vehicle's serial numbers, the clerk will issue new ownership papers.

The next stop is the license plate office. If license

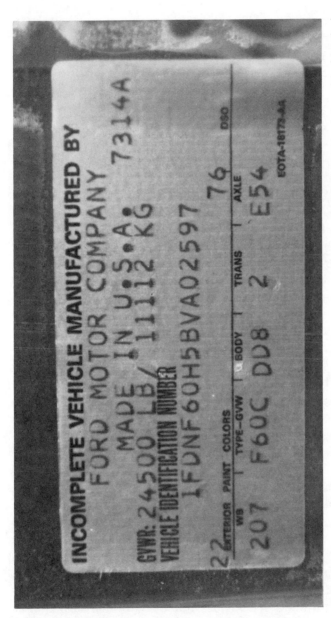

The VIN plate in over-the-road trucks is mounted on the driver's door or on the frame on the driver's side. When duplicating trucks, care must be taken to re- place rivets holding the VIN plate with identical matches to avoid detection.

plates were on the wrecked truck when it was purchased from the salvage dealer, they are changed into
the name of the new owner as it appears on the registration papers. If license plates were not on the vehicle
when it was purchased, they are issued in the name of
the new owner.

The thief then searches the streets for a truck identical to the one he purchased at the salvage yard. Any
1979 Freightliner cabover with sleeper and tandem axles
will not do. Each make of truck has five or six models
which, at first glance, appear to be the same, but are
not. The wheelbase and the sleeper width may vary only
one or two inches between the different models, but if
the thief does not exactly match the model listed on the
registration papers, a person who is knowledgeable
about trucks may spot the discrepancy and expose the
changeover.

Once an identical truck is located, it is stolen and
driven to a garage for the changeover. The first thing the
thief will do is remove the license plates and replace
them with those from the wrecked truck, or the new
ones he purchased. The VIN plate is then removed from
the door of the stolen truck and the VIN plate from the
wrecked truck is carefully installed with the same kind
of rivets as those that were removed.

The next step differs from the process of automobile conversion. Although it is rarely necessary or
wise to paint a stolen auto, it is necessary to paint a converted truck because it will be hunted actively over a
large area. Insurance companies tend to become highly
upset when a sixty-thousand-dollar truck disappears.
The police will probably think the truck is being used to
steal a trailer full of goodies, and there is nothing like re-
covering a hijacked truck to put stars on their caps.

Painting a truck does not draw undue suspicion as

does repainting an auto with a perfect paint job. If the paint job is not done by an accomplice, the thief will tell the owner of the paint shop he is leasing his truck to a new company and is required to have it painted in accordance with the company colors and design. Or, he will tell the painter he has ceased to work for a certain company and therefore no longer wants his truck to wear their colors. It is not unusual for an independent owner-operator to want his own special paint scheme. A new paint job also adds value to the truck when sold.

Presto! The wrecked truck has now been reincarnated and is ready for sale or lease to a company or to be driven by an owner-operator.

A converted truck can be detected as stolen if the engine, transmission or frame numbers are checked. But those who deal in and drive trucks know this will never happen unless someone points out the truck as stolen, or it is insured and involved in an accident where the owner tries to collect total value or replacement.

The Glider Kit Method

When a heavy-duty truck is wrecked in its current year of production, for instance a 1982 model wrecked during the year 1982, an insurance company will very seldom declare and sell the truck as salvage. This is due to the manner in which most trucks are wrecked.

Let's say, for example, that in January 1982, a 1982 model Ford 9000 is involved in a head-on collision with another vehicle. The cab of the truck is so damaged and the frame so twisted, it cannot be repaired. Instead of selling the truck for salvage, as in the case of a severely damaged auto, the insurance company will purchase a glider kit from the company who manufactured the damaged truck.

A *glider kit* consists of the frame, front axle and suspension, steering mechanism, completely assembled cab and sleeper, if the model has one, wiring, and all interior furnishings. Although the truck is not complete, a new bill of origin is issued with the glider kit and a new title can be obtained.

Glider kits are produced and sold by every heavy-duty truck manufacturer. Available for models only during their current production year, glider kits cannot be purchased for any make or model once it's out of production.

When an insurance company buys a glider kit, the kit and wrecked truck are taken to a garage and the motor, transmission, rear axles, suspension, and fifth wheel are removed from the wrecked truck and installed on the glider kit. The conversion takes approximately two hundred man-hours.

The bill of origin is then taken to the state registration or title office and registered as a new, previously unregistered truck.

Thieves have found the glider kit method useful because if a glider kit is completed with stolen parts, a title can easily be secured and the vehicle sold as a new truck. But since glider kits cost about twenty-five thousand dollars for top-of-the-line models, only sincere professionals have entered the business.

For the few thieves who have invested in glider kit conversions, the profits are high and the risks low. They will first purchase a glider kit for a popular model which can be easily sold. A title and registration papers are secured and license plates are bought.

A new truck, with running gear that will interchange with predrilled mountings on the glider kit, is then stolen. The engine and transmission are removed and their internal parts are removed and installed in new, unnumbered blocks and cases. All necessary parts and the unnumbered engine and transmission are installed and the conversion completed. License plates are installed and the truck is ready for sale.

Most thieves who are into truck conversion via the glider kit method have criminal connections for selling the cab and other parts they do not use to complete the kit. If they cannot find an outlet for these parts, they will be destroyed or saved for rebuilding a damaged truck that has not been totaled.

The Steal-Strip-Purchase-Repair Method

The steal-strip-purchase-repair method that works so well on auto conversion is favored even more by the truck thief. He realizes that the cost of converting a truck is only from one thousand to fifteen hundred dollars more than the price of converting an automobile, while the profit can be as much as fifty thousand dollars more per job.

The procedure for this method of truck conversion is the same as for the changeover of an auto. A truck is stolen and stripped of all parts, except the driver's side door. This door is left intact because it contains the VIN plate and the thief does not want to chance losing the plate before he can purchase the truck. Besides, it would look suspicious to steal the door and leave the VIN plate behind.

After the truck is stripped, the numbered engine block and transmission case are exchanged for new, unnumbered ones. The stripped hull is then bought from a salvage dealer and rebuilt with the parts which were previously removed from it.

The title and registration are changed to the name of

the new owner, license plates are bought and placed on the rebuilt truck, and the conversion is complete.

Duplicating Trucks

Duplicating trucks is almost unheard of, but it can and does happen. The procedure follows exactly that used for duplicating autos, with one exception: obtaining the VIN plate.

Since truck VIN plates are located on the driver's door and always exposed, a thief must be a real professional to exactly duplicate this plate.

I did know a thief once, however, who found a way of getting around this obstacle. Instead of using the plate he produced on the vehicle he stole, he would steal the VIN plate from the truck he wanted to duplicate, and replace it with the fake VIN plate he had prepared. The owner wouldn't notice the plate was a fake because he had no need to look closely at it.

The stolen plate would then be placed on the stolen truck so it could be sold. The stolen registration was taken to the state registration office and changed to the name he wished to use when selling the truck.

Trucks in title states are duplicated less often than trucks in nontitle states because very few trucks are fully paid for, and a clear title cannot be obtained. It is possible to title trucks from nontitle states in the more lax title states by duplicating them in the same manner autos are duplicated.

— — — — — — — — — — — — — — — —

To keep thieves from using the glider kit method of conversion, states could restrict the sale of glider kits to insurance companies and trucking firms, and require the submission of invoices for all parts used before a title would be issued.

If a truck is converted by any method and kept for personal use instead of sold, the culprit will most likely be an owner-operator. Since these truckers maintain their own rigs and seldom take them into commercial shops for minor repairs, stolen parts will likely go undetected.

The owner-operator is also the most likely recipient of converted trucks, knowingly or unknowingly. Even with the warning signs that a truck is a converted vehicle, he often does not *want* to know the true history of the vehicle. If he can get a clear title at a price he can afford to pay, he is often too happy to not ask questions.

10 Motorcycle Conversion

In most parts of the world, motorcycles have long been considered an economical, dependable, and primary means of transportation. In America, however, motorcycles have been looked upon primarily as recreational vehicles and symbols of nonconformity ridden by outlaw motorcycle gangs in open defiance of the traditional values of society.

But with gasoline and auto prices continuing to spiral upward, the public is taking a second look at the practicality of cycles. Anything that attracts the public's attention and demand will inevitably attract thieves as well.

Motorcycle conversion is not new. The reason it has not been more popular in the past is that the prices of motorcycles have remained low, making the process hardly worth the thief's while. This has changed. The new, larger, more expensive breeds of motorcycles on the market today commonly cost from three thousand to five thousand dollars.

Changeover methods for converting a motorcycle are markedly different from those used for converting an auto. Perhaps the biggest difference is that the salvage

On some motorcycles the VIN is both stamped into the frame and embossed onto a metal plate that is attached to the frame, making changing the number a doubly difficult job.

yard method is unfeasible; there are virtually no totally wrecked motorcycles with titles to be found.

When a motorcycle is involved in an accident in which it is severely damaged, it is always more cheaply repaired than replaced. After all, only so many parts on a cycle can be damaged. The engine, the biggest and most expensive part, is never totally damaged in an accident unless it is run over by a train or a bulldozer.

The steal-strip-purchase-repair method does work for motorcycle conversion, except that it is next to impossible to buy just the frame bearing the VIN and get the title and registration papers. If this is the chosen manner of conversion, however, the thief follows the same procedure for the steal-strip-purchase-repair method for autos. The engine block and transmission case are likewise exchanged.

Duplicating Motorcycles

Cycle owners seldom keep the registration for the cycle on the cycle; they keep it in their billfolds. A thief wanting to duplicate a certain motorcycle cannot simply steal the registration and take it to the tag office and purchase new license plates. Instead, he selects a model he wants, writes down the license number, then goes to the registration office to report that he has lost his pink slip. The clerk will research the records, run a check through NCIC, and issue a new or duplicate copy.

The thief will wait a week or so, then return to the registration office and report his license plate lost. The clerk will check the records, run the NCIC check, and issue new license plates and registration. With the license plates and registration complete, he will select and steal a motorcycle exactly like the one registered.

But there is a difficult part. Motorcycles do not have

VIN plates, only Vehicle Identification Numbers stamped into the frame. The old number must be removed from the stolen cycle and the VIN that appears on the registration papers must be stamped in.

Grinding off the number until it can no longer be seen is a method often used, but not by professionals. Grinding leaves an uneven surface in the area of the VIN and can also leave marks from the grinder.

Professionals first braze over the old number with a welding torch until the numbers are completely covered by the weld. Then the weld is ground down to the level of the metal and the edges feathered with a finer grinding disk to blend the weld with the frame. If the frame has a rough finish, as most do, a rock can be placed against the area that has been ground and tapped lightly with a hammer to restore the finish to its original condition.

The new VIN is stamped carefully into the frame and the area damaged by the welding and grinder is repainted the proper color. When the paint dries, rubbing compound is used to rub it out to blend with the old paint.

If the thief wants to be absolutely sure he will be safe when he sells the motorcycle, he will also buy new, unnumbered cases for the engine and transmission and make the exchange.

The new license plates are then installed and, in a nontitle state, the motorcycle is ready for sale. In a title state, the title must be secured in the same manner as for a duplicated auto. More motorcycles are paid for than automobiles, however, so finding one with a clear title is much easier. If only a few hundred dollars is owed on a cycle that can be sold for several thousand dollars, the thief may pay off the balance to obtain the clear title.

Motorcycle Chop Shops

The most common conversion for motorcycles is done by using the parts of a stolen cycle to repair a legal one that has been damaged. Since motorcycle parts have few numbers that can be traced, and since cycles can be easily stolen, chop shops that deal strictly in cycle parts are an increasingly popular and profitable part of the changeover industry.

These chop shops differ from auto chop shops in several ways. Motorcycles do not require a large garage for dismantling and storing parts. Most shops are housed in the garages of single-family homes, barns, and even the back rooms or workshops of motorcycle shops. When operated in motorcycle repair shops or dealerships, chop shops don't draw suspicion, since it's not unusual to see a cycle being taken apart. Everyone assumes it will also be put back together.

Cycle gangs are infamous for buying old motorcycles complete with titles and registration, stealing other cycles, and using their parts to rebuild the old, legal bikes. The manufacturers tend to make this all too easy. If there were more numbered parts on the cycles, there would be less theft of cycles for parts.

One of the main ways of selling stolen motorcycle parts is through newspaper ads. There are people who steal one cycle at a time, strip it, discard the frame, engine and transmission cases, and run an ad in the local papers or cycle magazines to sell the parts. The ad might read "Parting out 1979 Kawasaki 750, many good parts, make offer" and include the address or phone number. In a large city where motorcycles are popular, these thieves make a couple thousand dollars a week.

Good title and salvage laws would stop most conversions of motorcycles. However, since most cycles
are stolen for their parts and not for conversion through
use of the title and registration, this is a problem which
warrants serious consideration by manufacturers. Until
all parts are numbered and those numbers recorded in
case of theft, the stealing of cycles for their parts will
remain a lucrative business for thieves.

11 Camper and Trailer Conversion

Camping and travel trailers, those boxy-looking vehicles that allow people to escape in relative comfort for a weekend in the wilderness, or carry their lodging on vacation, are the easiest vehicles for a thief to convert. This is due primarily to their limited number of serial numbers and the laxity of state laws governing their registration and titling.

Conversion of these vehicles is by one of only two methods duplicating and securing title or registration by the use of false documents. The salvage yard method cannot be used because there are no totally wrecked travel trailers in salvage yards. They are too difficult to severely damage and too inexpensively repaired to warrant totaling.

The steal-strip-purchase-repair method does not work either, since there are no expensive exterior or drive train parts that can be removed. If the interior is stripped out, it can be reinstalled more cheaply than the entire vehicle can be replaced.

Conversion In Nontitle States

Some states with strict title laws for automobiles, trucks, and motorcycles have no title laws for camper and travel trailers. Therefore they will be included in this nontitle state conversion section.

In the majority of states not requiring titles for campers, it is very simple to obtain registration papers for these vehicles. A thief may merely carry a notarized bill of sale to the state registration office and ask for registration papers. The clerk may or may not run a check of the VIN through NCIC, depending on the policy of that state, and will then issue registration papers that may list the make, year, model, size, number of axles, weight, and VIN number.

In other states, only the weight and number of axles are listed on the registration. No VIN number is listed. In still other states, only the VIN and number of axles are listed.

In the case of theft and conversion, the thief will take to the state registration office a fake, notarized bill of sale, listing the make, model, year, size, weight, and number of axles of the type of vehicle he wishes to convert, as well as the nonexistent VIN he will put on the vehicle after it is stolen. If a check is run on the VIN number, it will come back clean, since there has never been a vehicle registered in that number. Registration papers will then be issued and the thief can take the papers to the license plate office and purchase license plates.

A vehicle identical to the one listed on the bill of sale and registration papers is then stolen and garaged for the actual conversion. The license plates are removed and replaced by the newly purchased ones.

The final step is to change the VIN number. Unlike

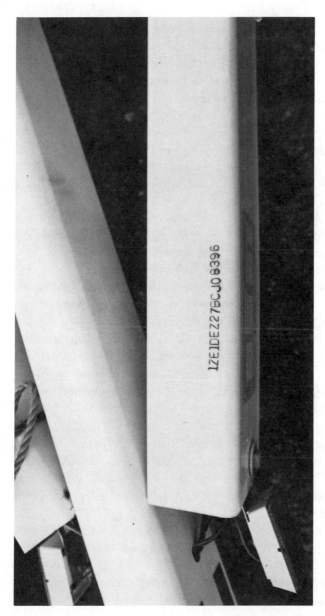

The VIN for camping and travel trailers is stamped onto the left side of the tongue midway between the hitch and the trailer body. The old numbers are oblit- erated then welded over before new, legitimate VIN numbers are stamped on.

automobiles and trucks, camping and travel trailers do not have a VIN plate. Their Vehicle Identification Numbers are located on the left side of the tongue, midway between the hitch and the body of the trailer. The number is stamped, not embossed, into the top side of the tongue in three-quarter-inch numerals.

Before the new number can be stamped in, the old number must be removed. Since the numbers are stamped fairly deeply, grinding them off is impractical and foolish. The metal would have to be ground so deeply to remove the indentations completely that the surface would be distorted even if the edges were feathered. Unless the metal were ground out to a depth of three-sixty-fourths of an inch below the bottom of the indentation caused by the stamping of the numbers, the numbers could be made visible again by saturating the area with a special acid. With this method, police are able to revive numbers that have been ground off.

The professional method of removing numbers is to first use a sharp punch and hammer to obliterate the old numbers. This destroys the molecules of metal that have been displaced by the stamping process and makes it impossible for the image of the numbers to be brought back after they have been removed.

An acetylene or arc welder will weld beads over the numbers, after which the weld is ground flush with the metal and the edges feathered to blend in. A rock is then placed over the ground area and tapped with a hammer until the surface matches the rest of the tongue.

The VIN is stamped into the tongue with the appropriate size and style of numbers and the area is spray painted to match the original color. To avoid spot painting problems, such as discoloration of the refinished area, the entire tongue can be painted.

The conversion is complete once the thief has registration papers that match the camper trailer, license plates that are properly registered to it, and a VIN on the trailer that appears on the registration papers. The merchandise can either be used as if it were legitimate, which for all means and purposes it now is, or be sold. Most conversions are placed for sale.

Conversion In Title States

Converting a camper or travel trailer in a title state is not impossible, but difficult, since more documents are needed to obtain the title than to secure registration in nontitle states. Trailers registered in nontitle states that are being registered and titled in title states are the exceptions. In these cases, trailers and their papers are subject to the same close scrutiny as an automobile from these states and the procedure for titling is the same.

To receive a title for a trailer unregistered in a title state, the thief must produce a bill of origin and a bill of sale. The bill of origin is the most difficult to obtain and since it cannot be readily purchased, the thief will need a cooperative printer to produce fakes from an original.

The fake bill of origin is filled out for a camper of the make and model the thief intends to convert, exactly as the manufacturer would fill out a legitimate bill of origin for a newly produced camper trailer. The space for the VIN is filled in with a nonexistent number.

A bill of sale is printed on the letterhead stationery of a well-established recreational vehicle dealer and filled out. The price of the camper trailer is listed "paid in cash," so there will be no lien held against it.

The bill of origin and bill of sale can be taken to the state title office and registered as a new, previously unregistered vehicle. Because the VIN listed in the bill of origin and bill of sale does not actually exist, it will not be listed with NCIC as stolen. Since the bill of sale states that full payment has been made by the new owner, a clear title will be issued. With the registration papers in hand, the thief goes to the license plate office and purchases new license plates.

The preliminaries completed, the thief is ready to steal a matching camper trailer and goes about changing the VIN as described earlier. When this step is accomplished, the vehicle is ready for sale or use.

Duplicating In Nontitle States

The first problem encountered in duplicating a camping or travel trailer in a nontitle or title state is getting registration papers since they are seldom kept with the vehicle. The thief must first go to the vehicle registration office and report his registration papers lost. The clerk will issue new registration papers in the name of the rightful owner for the camper trailer he has selected.

He then goes to the license plate registration office and reports the license plate lost. After an NCIC check, the clerk will issue new license plates and a new tag receipt, again in the name of the rightful owner. A bill of sale is prepared as if the vehicle was sold by the rightful owner to the name indicated by the thief, and is notarized.

The bill of sale and registration papers are taken back to the registration office or, preferably, to another registration office, and new registration papers issued in the name of the new owner listed on the bill of sale. The license plates are also changed to the new name.

A trailer identical to the one that was registered is then stolen and the VIN is changed to match the registration papers. The license plates that were on the stolen trailer are removed and new ones installed. The duplicating is complete and the vehicle ready for sale.

Duplicating In Title States

Securing a title for duplicating a camping or travel trailer in a title state is done in the same manner as for any other vehicle. The thief must first find a trailer that has a clear title. He then reports the title lost and requests a duplicate title. When he has the title, he reports the license plate registration lost and receives new registration papers in the name of the rightful owner.

He then reports his license plates lost and receives new license plates and registration papers in the name of the rightful owner.

A bill of sale is made out in the name the thief wishes to register the vehicle, as if it were bought from the actual owner. It is then notarized and taken with the title and registration papers to the title office. The papers are processed just as any legitimate transaction would be and the thief receives a title and registration papers in the name he has chosen.

An identical vehicle is then stolen, its license plates replaced with the new plates, the old VIN number removed, and the new number, which appears on the title and registration papers, stamped in its place. The conversion is complete and the trailer is ready for sale.

If a trailer is duplicated in a nontitle state and brought to a title state for titling and registering, it must face the same scrutiny as an automobile must. But if the numbers have been meticulously and properly altered, they can stand close examination and the thief will have no problem.

— — — — — — — — — — — — — — — —

The problem of preventing travel and camper trailer conversion is twofold. First, state law governing the registration of these vehicles is unbelievably lax in construction making enforcement impossible. Secondly, vehicle manufacturers should devise better means of placing the VIN. If it was embossed in the tongue, instead of stamped on it, it would be very difficult to change.

The lack of factory-installed antitheft devices on trailers warrants attention. There are no locks on trailers to prevent thieves from simply backing up to them, hooking up the hitches, and pulling them away. No other vehicle is so easy to steal.

12 Boat Conversion

Boats are the most difficult vehicles to detect as stolen once they are converted, since small boats lack manufacturer's serial numbers and the numbers on large boats can easily be changed. Furthermore, most states do not require boats to be titled and registered in the same manner as automobiles.

Depending on state laws, a boat may be required to be registered in one of three places. In nontitle states, boats are sometimes registered with the Fish and Game Department. Other nontitle states may require boats to be registered with the Department of Motor Vehicles in the same manner that automobiles are registered. In title states which require the titling of boats, they are titled and registered through the same procedure as automobiles are. However, some title states do not require boats and other nonmotorized vehicles to be titled, only registered.

Boats differ from all other vehicles in that they are not assigned their serial numbers at the time they are manufactured. The VIN is assigned and issued by the state in which they are registered, at the time of registration. These numbers consist of two letters, which are

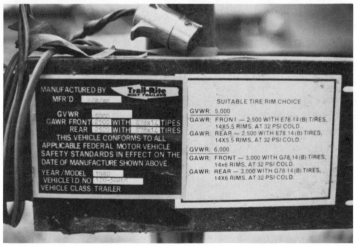

Stolen boats are not easily detected since some larger boats have VIN numbers and most smaller ones do not. The number painted on the bow is the state registration number. The VIN on boat trailers are either stamped into the metal frame or onto a plate.

the abbreviation for that state (*FL* for Florida, *CA* for California, *NY* for New York, etc.), followed by five or six numerals. For example, a boat registered in Florida might bear the registration number *FL 736191.*

This registration number remains the same as long as the boat is registered in that state, no matter how many times it changes ownership. If the owner moves to another state, the old registration number is removed and the new state letters and numbers put on.

When the registration number is issued by the state, the three-inch high, self-adhesive letters and numbers are given to the owner for installation. Some states allow the owner to paint the registration numbers on the boat instead of sticking on the issued numbers. In all states, the registration number is installed on the upper bow on both sides of the boat.

Methods of boat conversion are as varied as those used in automobile conversion, but are no more complicated. The salvage method, steal-strip-purchase-repair method, duplicating, and conversion can each be used to make a boat seem legitimate.

The Salvage Method

Anyone who has ever walked through a boatyard or marina has seen the rusting, decaying hulls of boats bobbing in the wake and tilting in drydock. These boats can be bought and converted in the same manner as autos purchased from a salvage yard with one big exception: The stolen boat does not have to be the exact year as the salvaged boat, or even the exact make. It must, however, be the same type of boat. For example, if the salvaged boat is a twenty-one-foot V-bottom, a twenty-one-foot tunnel-hull or flat-bottom will not match. A bass boat will not be acceptable as a replacement for a cabin cruiser of the same length, even though the shape of the hull is the same. When dealing with boats under twenty-five feet in length, it is next to impossible to tell a 1975 nineteen-foot V-bottom from a 1980 nine-teen-foot V-bottom.

As an example, let's say that a thief finds a seven-teen-foot runabout that has been run aground in a marina. There is a big hole in the port side of the hull and all usable parts including the engine have been removed. Such a boat can be bought for a couple hundred dollars, and since there are no salvage laws governing the boat industry, the title and registration papers come with the boat.

The thief first changes the ownership of the boat to the name he will use when selling the boat after its conversion, and destroys the remainder of the boat. An identical type of boat is then stolen. The numbers are removed from the bow and the new numbers which appear on the registration papers are installed in their place.

On a boat having an identification plate *and* numbers on the bow, the plate is removed from the salvage boat and placed on the stolen one. These plates are always attached with rivets and can be removed and replaced in the same manner as those on automobiles. They are usually located on the control center of the captain's station, but location may vary on different makes and models.

If a thief cannot find the kind of boat he wishes to convert, he may steal and destroy a boat like the one he wants, then buy it when it is sold at salvage. In these cases, the boat is usually burned. The thief knows that if there is an identification plate, it will not be harmed by the fire and the numbers on the bow must be replaced anyway.

The Steal-Strip-Purchase-Repair Method

The steal-strip-purchase-repair method works just as well for boats as it does for autos if the boat's hull is damaged as well. Stripping the boat is not enough in itself to warrant it being declared totaled by an insurance company. Although removable parts are expensive, they can be reinstalled for less than the entire boat can be replaced. So the thief will knock a hole in the hull and sink the craft in shallow water where it can be recovered without too much trouble. The location of the hull is reported to the police or coast guard, who will in turn notify the insurance company. After the insurance company surveys the damage, they will be all too happy to sell it for salvage and surrender all claim and papers. The thief then refloats the boat, has the hull repaired, and reinstalls the parts he earlier removed. It is then ready for sale.

Boat Duplicating In Nontitle States

Duplicating a boat in a nontitle state follows exactly the same procedure used to duplicate camping and travel trailers, except changing the numbers. If the thief is planning to use a stolen trailer with the converted boat, the trailer must also be duplicated. But most thieves will buy a used trailer for a couple hundred dollars instead of going to the trouble of duplicating one. The legitimate trailer will give them a better set of papers and is cheap insurance against having a stolen boat exposed by the discovery of a duplicated trailer.

To duplicate the boat, the thief selects a boat like the one he will convert, copies the registration number from the bow, and goes to the appropriate office to report his papers lost. Registration papers are issued to him in the name of the rightful owner. If the boat is to be sold in the name of the real owner, the paperwork is complete.

If the boat is to be sold under another name, the thief will make out a bill of sale from the real owner to the name he intends to use, have it notarized, and carry it and the registration papers to the state registration office where the ownership will be changed into the name appearing on the bill of sale.

There are no license plates to purchase and register since boats do not have license plates; only their trailers have license plates.

A matching boat is stolen, and the numbers are removed from the bow, and replaced with the numbers which appear on the registration papers. If the boat also has an identification plate, it is removed and duplicated. If the boat which is being duplicated is not in use, its identification plate may be removed and placed on the stolen boat. The boat then has the real identification plate and numbers that coincide with those on the registration papers and can be sold.

Boat Duplicating In Title States

Boat duplicating in title states is done the same way any other vehicle is duplicated in those states. The thief must determine that the boat he will duplicate has a clear title and secure that title. The registration must also be secured and, if necessary or desired, changed into the name in which it will be sold.

The boat is converted in the same manner as those in nontitle states.

Boat trailers are titled and registered in title states just as travel trailers are. But boat trailers are inexpensive and hardly worth the problems incurred in conversion and duplicating. The thief realizes most people think that if the trailer is properly registered, the boat will be also. It never occurs to them that, although the four-hundred-dollar trailer is legal, the eight-thousand-dollar boat it carries is a changeover.

Boat Conversion

Some thieves do not go to the trouble of salvaging previously registered boats, stealing, stripping, purchasing, and repairing them, or even duplicating them. They merely obtain false documents and use them to secure legal registration papers and titles. They then steal a boat, attach the appropriate numbers and registration plates, and come up with boats they can sell, use, or re-register forever.

Converting a stolen boat follows exactly the procedure used for securing papers for a travel trailer both in the title and nontitle states. The numbers are changed as described earlier.

— — — — — — — — — — — — — — — —

As with camping and travel trailers, it is obvious that manufacturers and state laws make it far too easy to convert a stolen boat to one which can be legitimized and sold. Boats are unregulated by salvage laws, allowing them to be sold and rebuilt regardless of their condition. Insurance companies, anxious to recover as much of the loss as possible, readily sell the boat as salvage. Apparently they don't realize that by selling the boat, complete with papers, as salvage, they will likely have to pay for a boat that will be stolen and converted with the registration from the boat they sold.

13 Airplane Conversion

Converting stolen airplanes into legitimate transportation, a practice virtually unheard of a few years ago, is occurring with increasing frequency. The majority of conversions are for temporary use and often related to the transport of drugs. Aircraft stolen for changeover range from Piper Cubs to Lear Jets. The manner of conversion may be any of those used to convert an automobile, but duplicating is the most likely.

The various methods of salvage conversion are seldom used, except when a plane is intended for personal use, since an inspection and certificate of airworthiness are required before a damaged plane can be flown. Aircraft involved in an accident are thoroughly investigated by FAA investigators, who file their report with the Civil Aeronautic Board. Before the plane can be put back into service, it is supposedly inspected and a new certificate of airworthiness issued.

If a thief is able to obtain registration papers for a damaged aircraft, he can simply steal an identical airplane, have it repainted to cover the old numbers on the fuselage, and the new registration numbers painted in their place. He cannot sell the plane because a check of

Airplanes receive a number comparable to the VIN from the Federal Aviation Agency. The number on a stolen plane is changed by simply painting on a new number.

FAA records by a prospective buyer would reveal that a plane with those registration numbers had been totally damaged at one time. Federal Aviation Agency investigators sent out to issue a certificate of airworthiness would undoubtedly learn the plane is stolen.

If the thief does not try to sell the aircraft, however, and avoids large airports which might have FAA personnel asking to see its certificate of airworthiness and maintenance records, the plane might go undetected for years.

The most popular method for airplane conversion is duplicating. Unlike automobile duplicating, airplane duplicating does not require a visit by the thief to registration offices for registration papers and license plates. Also, unlike other vehicles, airplanes are duplicated for personal use, not for sale. Due to the high cost of aircraft, it is difficult to find a fully-paid-for plane. The registration of a plane with a lien holder would not clear the FAA if the thief tried to sell the aircraft.

Airplane duplicating also follows a different procedure than other kinds of duplicating. First, the thief rents or leases an airplane for a week or month. While the aircraft is in his possession, he duplicates all registration papers, the airworthiness certificate, and the maintenance records. The rental or lease agreement is also duplicated, and the rental or lease period is listed as one year, the usual time period for a longterm lease. Having served its purpose, the rental craft is returned to the agency from which it was rented.

An identical aircraft is then located, stolen, and flown to a hangar where it will be converted. The theft usually takes place in a city several thousand miles from the area where it will be used. Most thieves will go to Canada, Mexico, or South America to steal the plane, since a plane stolen from one of these countries will not be sought so actively in the U.S.

Because the true identity of an airplane will never escape detection under a thorough inspection and investigation, only two changes are made on the stolen airplane: the FAA registration number painted on the fuselage, and the hour meter which records the operating time of the aircraft.

Having the aircraft repainted and the numbers redone requires the cooperation of a painter who will know he is violating the law. Aircraft are given their registration numbers by the FAA. They are painted on by the manufacturer and are never changed regardless of how many times the aircraft changes ownership or how many times it is repainted. No reputable aircraft painter will risk having his license revoked, or going to jail, for changing the registration numbers of an airplane.

A stolen airplane is seldom totally repainted. If the plane is red and white, for example, the red part will usually be painted blue. If it is done properly, the paint job will exactly match the color pattern of the rented plane that is being duplicated.

The hour meter is changed only when the plane is going to be kept so long that it might require maintenance. The mechanic who fills out the maintenance record may become suspicious if the meter lists less time than when the plane was last maintained or several thousand hours more than is required for routine maintenance.

Once the registration numbers have been duplicated and the hour meter adjusted to match that of the rental aircraft, the thief will take the plane to a small airport, rent a pad or tie-down space, and use the airport as a base of operation. Since he has the lease agreement, registration papers, and the airplane to match, the

Fixed Base Operator will not be suspicious.

Airplane duplicating for personal use, not sale, is without a doubt the most difficult form of duplicating to detect. There are no routine traffic checks as with other vehicles, no license plates to purchase and renew, no title and registration offices to visit, and if an accident occurs, the thief will probably not survive to be prosecuted.

Of all the airplane duplications I have known about or been involved in, only one led to apprehension. A stolen duplicate and the original airplane both landed at the same airport at the same time and met at the fuel pumps. The attendant did not notice that both planes bore the same numbers until after the stolen duplicate had departed. He then contacted the control tower operator who checked the thief's flight plan. Police arrested him when he landed at his destination. Had he been operating the plane farther from the area where the plane he duplicated was stationed and operating, he might still be in business.

14 Protecting Dealership Vehicles

Although automotive and recreational vehicle dealerships are seldom recipients of converted vehicles, they are frequently the targets of thieves. At dealerships thieves can quickly find the exact vehicles they want, steal them at night, on the weekend, or a holiday, and change them over before they are missed and reported stolen.

Automotive Dealership Theft Prevention

There are two kinds of auto dealerships: open lots and closed lots. Open lots have no barrier of any kind to prevent visitors from driving in or out after the dealership is closed. Closed lots have some type of barrier which does not permit entry or exit of vehicles after hours.

Although open lots create a sense of friendliness by allowing people to come in and browse after hours, they also invite thieves to drive off with the auto of their choice.

Even some closed lots do not have effective barriers. A curb along the front row of cars can be easily driven over. A cable or chain stretched across the entry is a deterrent, but if it is too high or too loose, it can be driven under. If it is made of light-duty material, it can be cut with bolt cutters. Other autos or trucks parked to block entrances and exits can be unlocked and moved in the same way the desired vehicle will be stolen.

The best precautionary step a dealership can take is to cement four-foot lengths of four-inch-diameter pipe into the ground to a depth of two feet. The pipe is set at four-foot intervals around the property where a vehicle could be driven away, then filled with cement. The cement will keep the thief from using a pipe cutter on the barrier, then driving over it.

A heavy anchor chain like the kind used on large ships should be used to secure entries and exits. The chain should be welded to a post on one side and fastened to a post on the other side with a heavy padlock. If it is stretched across openings at a height of two feet, it will be too high to drive over and too low to drive under. Heavy-duty chains and padlocks cannot be easily cut.

A professional thief never needs a key to enter and start an automobile, but if one is available he will, of course, use it. Dealers tend to make it far too easy for the thief to get keys for the vehicle he wants.

As an act of courtesy and for customer convenience, most dealers leave the keys to all vehicles in the ignition switches or over the sun visors. This practice makes it easy for the customer to check out any vehicle he chooses and gives the thief a key from which he can have another one made. Or he can simply take the key and substitute a fake key in its place.

If the vehicle has several keys on the key ring, the thief may remove the ignition key, which also opens the

Car dealerships can protect their vehicles from thieves by sinking concrete-filled pipes vertically into the ground and stringing heavy-weight chain between them to prevent entry and exit. This trusting dealer has taken no precautions, yet.

doors, and substitute another for the same make of vehicle. For example, if he removed a key from a Ford, he would replace it with a Ford key. Then if someone else tries to start the vehicle and finds the key does not fit the switch, he will think something is wrong with the key.

If the thief selects a vehicle with only one key on the key ring, he will ask a partner to take the key to a nearby key shop, have a duplicate made, and return the key to the vehicle before it is missed.

The best way a dealer can prevent key duplication and theft is by placing only one set of keys to a vehicle on a ring large enough to be seen from a distance, and leaving it in the lock of the driver's door. Then lot salespersons can see at a glance if all the keys are with the vehicles.

When the keys are retrieved in the evening, *all* keys should be tried in the locks to assure they are the right keys. If one or more does not fit, a switch has been made and a theft is imminent.

Most thefts from dealerships are made shortly after they close or on weekends during the daylight hours, rather than at one o'clock in the morning. If the dealership closes at six in the evening, the thief will likely strike as soon as the last employee leaves. Then if anyone sees him leaving with an auto, it will appear he is a salesman driving one of the demos.

If the theft takes place on Sunday or a holiday, it will probably be planned for in the morning while people are in church or sleeping late.

A dealer can gain some protection by asking businesspersons near his car lot to watch for suspicious characters when the establishment is closed. Times when theft is most likely to occur should be pointed out.

Recreational Vehicle Dealership Theft Protection

Recreational vehicle dealerships are often located outside of the city to create a better atmosphere for sale. The location also creates a better atmosphere for theft. Recreational vehicle dealers can take preventive measures auto dealers use plus one more: They can remove the wheels from vehicles on their lots.

Since recreational vehicles are not taken for a ride around the block by potential buyers like autos are, their wheels can be removed and stored in another location or a building equipped with a burglar alarm. Although this is a simple, inexpensive means of prevention, it is almost totally effective. There are not many thieves who will go to the trouble and expense of buying wheels, tires, tubes, and lug nuts, have the tubes and tires mounted on the wheels, and then risk being seen when they are mounting the wheels on the trailer. Instead, they will pass up the dealership in favor of finding one who thought it too ridiculous to remove the wheels from the trailers.

Protection Against Buying A Conversion

Since there is always a chance a thief will try to sell a stolen and converted vehicle to a dealer, there are a few rules all dealerships should follow.

One person in each dealership should be trained to check out and purchase all vehicles from private parties. He or she should follow all the directives given to private buyers in chapter thirteen.

The dealer should never be content with just receiving a clean report from the title and registration office. The title and registration office cannot say whether or not the vehicle is stolen, only who owns it and if it is free of liens. A check with the police department should be made to insure that the vehicle is not stolen.

The foremost rule to remember is *never* take anything for granted, and *never assume* that the seller is telling is the truth.

15 Insurance Agents—A Line of Defense

Every time an insured vehicle is stolen, premiums for vehicle theft insurance climb a little higher. The public seems to accept, or at least agree with, the logic of increased risk translating into increased rates. However, I have found that the overzealous agents of many insurance companies seem more interested in writing policies for theft prevention than helping to stem it.

Since almost everyone who purchases a vehicle insures it, knowledgeable agents can help prevent theft by detecting stolen vehicles overlooked by the owners and financial institutions. If the theft is detected soon after the sale is made, chances are good the thief will be caught.

Insurance agents, like many others, accept things at face value and assume the information they are given is correct. They assume the vehicle is the one listed on the registration papers. They assume the VIN corresponds with other serial numbers on the vehicle. They assume the entire vehicle is intact. They assume the owner bought the vehicle from a legitimate party. They assume the seller was the rightful owner of the vehicle and acquired it by legal means.

If an agent assumes any or all of the above without further investigation when he is writing a policy, he is leaving himself open to insuring a stolen vehicle. This can be a very costly mistake. Here are some examples.

For a two-year period, I bought hulls of totally wrecked automobiles from salvage yards, complete with titles and registration papers. As soon as I was in possession of the hulls, I destroyed everything except the VIN plate, title, and registration papers. I then filled out a false bill of sale, listing the previous owner as the seller and myself as the purchaser, notarized the document, and took it and the title and registration papers to the state title office where ownership was changed into my name. I then went to the Department of Motor Vehicles, bought license plates, and received proper registration. With the vehicle registered in my name, I went to an insurance agency, purchased full coverage including theft, and paid the first three months' premium.

In 90 percent of the cases, the insurance agents never asked to see the automobile. In the few cases they did request to see the vehicle, I told them that my wife had dropped me off at the agency and I would bring the auto back later. Usually they said that would not be necessary. If they did insist on my bringing it back, I stole an auto that matched my description, put on the license plates I had purchased, and replaced the VIN plate with the one from the wreck I had bought at the salvage yard. I then returned with that vehicle for inspection and verification.

I then removed the VIN plate and license plates from the automobile I had stolen to show the agent and abandoned it. In three or four weeks, I reported the automobile I had insured as stolen. Since there never was an auto which could be located, the insurance company promptly paid me the replacement price of the vehicle. Not once did insurance companies make a background check of the automobile before paying off the policy. I suppose they assumed their agents would be more careful than to insure a vehicle which was not actually a whole automobile.

While I was in this business, I averaged about three automobiles a month and never ran out of willing agents to write my policies, and pay off my claims.

Another game I used to play with insurance companies was to changeover an auto by the salvage yard method, but not bother with changing the engine and transmission cases. I then sold the vehicle to an unsuspecting party and determined whether or not they were covered by auto theft insurance. A week or so later, I stole the vehicle back and ran it through a chop shop. This way I never had to worry about anyone finding out the vehicle was stolen and tracing it back to me.

The people to whom I had sold the car simply filed a claim and the insurance bought another, legitimate automobile for them. Apparently it never occurred to the insurance companies or their agents that there was anything suspicious going on.

Another insurance sham I ran was to purchase an automobile which had been stripped by parts thieves. I registered the vehicle in my own name as any new owner would do. I then took the registration papers to an insurance agent and bought full coverage. A few weeks later, I took the stripped vehicle to an isolated area and dumped it. Then I reported it stolen.

If the police did not find it within a few days, I called them and anonymously told them where it was located. After the police recovered the auto and contacted me, I notified the insurance company. The company dispatched a claims adjuster to survey the damage and settle the claim. In every case the

auto was either restored to its original condition or replaced with a similar model. For my one thousand to
fifteen-hundred dollar investment, I was given an automobile worth between five thousand and fifteen thousand dollars, depending on the make and model I had
purchased at salvage.

To say that all of the insurance claims I collected for
stolen or stripped autos could have been prevented is an
understatement! These claims not only could have been
avoided, they *should* have been avoided. In not one
case would I have succeeded if the insurance agent had
bothered to check the background and other serial numbers of the autos before issuing a policy. If the claims
adjuster had double-checked the work of the agent who
sold the policy, he would have also detected the phony
claim.

Definite guidelines should be instituted for agents to
follow when writing policies and settling claims. Besides
following the directives for private buyers set forth in
chapter five, they should always include a visual examination of the vehicle!

Before a claim is settled for a stolen, stripped or
burnt vehicle, the claims adjuster should make the same
inquiries first, to double-check the findings of the agent
and, second, to make sure that the agent is not working
with the thief. I once dealt with an agent who, for two
hundred dollars, would insure anything I had the registration for, unseen, and without my coming into his
office.

It is unlikely that a thief will use the same agent or
company twice in a short period of time, unless the
agent is aware of the activities. But it does happen.
Agents and claims adjusters should constantly be alert
for the same name, or the same person using a different
name, showing up to collect on claims. In almost every

case, the vehicle will be a late model, and the theft will take place within four weeks of the date the policy was written.

The time to prevent false insurance claims is *before* the policy is written. After the vehicle has been reported stolen, there will be no way to prove that it was not legitimate and fully intact when it was insured. The insuring agent will certainly not admit that he wrote a policy for a vehicle he did not fully inspect, or at least see.

A good insurance agent can fully check a vehicle in five or six minutes, including making the necessary calls to the registration office and previous owner. Considering the average price of autos and other vehicles today, the savings could amount to more than one thousand dollars per minute if the vehicle is detected as a fake.

Although most false claims are for automobiles, they are equally possible for motorcycles, camping and travel trailers, trucks, vans, buses, and boats. All rules of prevention should be applied equally to all vehicles.

16 First Aid for Legal Loopholes

Title and registration personnel in state offices process thousands of vehicle registration papers each week until they become almost mechanical beings. The routine in these offices is so dismal that eventually all the papers and numbers and people who come to change and exchange them all look alike. This is especially true in large cities where the flow of paper is substantial.

In the past, I was in the same title and registration offices a dozen times in one week and used half as many names and no one seemed to notice or care. In their striving for efficiency, the clerks unwittingly aid changeover artists and the auto theft industry.

Clerks must remain alert and suspicious if the changeover artists are to be stopped. Although the personnel of these offices cannot detect duplicated, false, or otherwise unlawful conversions, they can learn to recognize patterns that can lead to detection.

The easiest pattern to recognize is the return of the same person again and again to have various vehicles titled and registered to himself or other people. It is not unusual for a person to occasionally register a vehicle for someone else who cannot visit the office. But when that person appears often, the clerk should know he is not merely a good Samaritan.

Another pattern thieves establish is registering several different vehicles in the names they are using. Even used car dealers do not do this. They leave the title and registration open to avoid paying taxes on the license plate, and, in some cases, to show less profit at the end of the year.

If questioned by a clerk, the thief will usually say he is a used car dealer. The clerk should then ask to see his business license or call his place of business to verify his claim. It is unlikely that a thief will have a dealer's license. Most states require all prospective vehicle dealers to be fingerprinted and their background investigated before a license can be issued. Operating as a dealer would leave a clear trail for authorities to follow to the thief in the event one of the changeovers was detected.

Clerks in title states should pay close attention to vehicles bought from nontitle states or title states without strict salvage laws. Thieves actually prefer to do business in title states rather than nontitle states because the title adds an air of authenticity and respectability to the transaction. Some states require nontitled vehicles to undergo inspections by the local police department, but most do not. Where they do not, the clerk should make inquiries on his own initiative.

A Good Title Law

No state in America has a title, registration, or salvage law that is not full of loopholes a thief can use to convert vehicles. The following outline may help "thief-proof" these laws based on my experiences with punching holes in them.

- All vehicles including boats and camper trailers should be titled.
- Only a licensed dealer should title a vehicle when it is titled for the *first* time. Before a title is issued, a check should be made with the manufacturer to assure the bill of origin is not a fake.
- Before license plates are issued, even including replacements for lost plates, the vehicle should be inspected by the police department and a check made of *all* serial numbers through NCIC.
- Lost registration papers and titles should be reissued by the registration and title office only after inspection and an NCIC check. The person to whom the replacement papers are issued should be required to establish his identity to the satisfaction of the title office personnel.
- Whenever ownership is changed from one party to another, the vehicle should undergo an inspection and serial number check through NCIC.
- Whenever a vehicle is involved in an accident, the title and registration of that vehicle should be surrendered until that vehicle is repaired. Invoices should be required to show where replacement parts were purchased, and an inspection and check of that vehicle conducted.
- When an insurance company sells a vehicle as salvage, all title and registration papers should be surrendered and destroyed. In the case of automobiles, boats, and trucks, the VIN plate should be surrendered and destroyed.
- Any vehicle sold as salvage should never, under *any* circumstances, be allowed back in operation.
- Glider kits should be sold only to licensed trucking firms and truck repair shops. When the repairs are completed, the rebuilder should produce invoices of all

parts used in the building. The vehicle should undergo an inspection and serial number check.

Conclusion

Auto theft is a multi-million dollar industry that lines the pockets of thieves at the expense of the persons who must make payments on uninsured vehicles that are stolen, who are out the money they unwittingly pay for stolen cars that are later discovered and confiscated, and who bear increased insurance premiums due to costs of replacement. Then there's the stress, unmeasurable in dollars, of the frustration, confusion, and time required to deal with stolen-vehicle problems.

But 98 percent of all changeovers could be prevented if some simple precautions were taken. If title and salvage laws were written as I have described in this book, and if personnel of title and registration departments and law officers performed their duties with an eye out for the stolen vehicle, the business of theft would languish.

The theft of cars, motorcycles, trucks, boats, airplanes, and travel trailers can never be completely stopped, however, because the use of stolen parts to rebuild legitimate vehicles can never be completely stopped. There will always be crooked salvage yard dealers willing to supply body shops with invoices, even for stolen parts. Chop shops will continue to profit on the sale of stolen doors, fenders, hoods, and the internal parts of engines and transmissions as long as car parts remain unnumbered by manufacturers.

The private buyer, however, the final line of defense, must always be alert for the stolen vehicle if he is to protect himself from being taken for a ride financially by a thief. Knowing what to look for both in the paper work and in the cosmetics of a vehicle is necessary if a buyer wants to make sure his new vehicle is legitimate.

The bottom line of the auto theft industry is that as long as it supplies thieves with money, it will flourish. It's the old law of supply and demand.